RETURN ⬮TO⬮ WONDER

*Recapture a Childlike Fascination
with Daily Life*

A GUIDEPOSTS BOOK BY
ARTHUR GORDON

BROADMAN
&HOLMAN
PUBLISHERS

NASHVILLE, TENNESSEE

Every attempt has been made to credit the sources of copyright material used in this book. If any such acknowledgment has been inadvertently omitted or miscredited, receipt of such information would be appreciated.

Devotional material from *Daily Guideposts* is copyright © 1982, 1984, 1985, 1986, 1987, 1989, 1990, 1991, 1992, 1994, 1995 by Guideposts, Carmel, NY 10512.

"The Power of Affection," January 1968; "Make Up Your Mind, Oreo!," February 1988; "A Mite Wicked," March 1992. Reprinted by permission from *Guideposts* Magazine. Copyright by Guideposts, Carmel, New York 10512.

"A Very Special Kind of Day" first appeared in *Field & Stream*, November 1991. Reprinted with permission.

William Butler Yeats excerpts are from *The Collected Poems of William Butler Yeats*. Reprinted by kind permission of A.P. Watt Ltd. on behalf of Anne Yeats.

RETURN TO WONDER

First Broadman & Holman edition, 1996.

Jacket design by Paz Design, Salem, Oregon

Designed by José R. Fonfrias
Printed in the United States of America

Contents

Introduction

DOWN IN GEORGIA where we live there is a tidal creek with an old dock not far from our house. I like to fish there now and then, or sometimes to just sit and watch the cloud-changes or the wind in the marshes.

Early one morning, close to sunrise, I found myself walking down the narrow path that leads to the dock. Trees crowd in on both sides, and suddenly I came to an abrupt halt facing an enormous spiderweb, gray and almost invisible, that stretched from one tree to another, completely blocking the path.

My first reaction was exasperation. I couldn't walk through such a large web; I would have to use something to brush it aside. So I retreated a few steps, looking for a stick, and finally found one. But as I turned again, the rising sun cleared the top of the marshes across the creek. Its rays flashed along the path so that now I saw in front of me, not a shadowy spiderweb, but a dew-spangled miracle of engineering hanging there, perfectly symmetrical, gleaming with diamonds, swaying gently in the soft wind. It was stunning. It was more than stunning; it was exquisite. Could this be the work of a mindless crawling creature? Could that creature be part of an Infinite Mind that chose to reveal itself in this extraordinary way?

I didn't disturb the web, I angled my way around it. When I reached the dock, still holding the stick, the impact lingered. I felt as if my own mind had been stretched by this unexpected encounter, stretched and filled with a combination of amazement and incredulity and awe that I hadn't felt for a long time. There was a name for this emotion, and I knew what it was. It was wonder.

Some years before, some decades in fact, I had written a book called *A Touch of Wonder*. The theme of the book was quite simple. It was the notion that life consists of an endless series of marvels, that even the most commonplace happenings are full of them, and that they will reveal themselves gladly to those who will take the trouble to pause and look and feel and care just a bit more than they usually do.

Part of this notion came from a friend of mine, a crusty old psychiatrist named Smiley Blanton. Smiley was convinced that a sense of wonder is a key element in emotional health. "It's not just a nice thing to have," he used to say. "It's one of the foundations of man's understanding of himself and his place in the universe. So reach out to anything that makes you feel wonder. Hold onto it. Cherish it. Never let it get away!"

So spoke my friend Smiley. But now, standing there on the

weathered planking of the old dock, I wondered if in recent months and years I had been guilty of letting it fade away. I looked at the stick with which I had come so close to brushing wonder aside. I let it drop into the creek and stared down at the green water.

In the book written so many years ago, I had a great deal to say about the importance of wonder. But I could recall no words of wisdom for those who found their awareness of it growing dim. Was there a remedy to offer such people? Was there, indeed, any advice I could give myself? What could I, what could anyone do to reawaken their sense of wonder?

"Return to it," said a small voice somewhere inside my head. "In *A Touch of Wonder* you dealt mostly with things in the present. Now you're much farther down the road, with countless memories behind you, hundreds of occasions where wonder was a counter balance to troubles or trials or disappointments or failures. These little luminous moments have been with you all the way. Try reaching back for some of them. Remembered wonder may make you realize once more how important it is. Start at the beginning and follow through to the almost-end. You still have time. . . ."

A small voice, but an insistent one. *Return to Wonder.* In the pages that follow that is what I am trying to do.

Out of the Mist

The most beautiful experience we can have is the mysterious. Whomever does not know it and can no longer wonder, no longer marvel, is as good as dead, and his eyes are dimmed.

Albert Einstein

IN HIS INTRODUCTION to *Through the Looking-Glass,* Lewis Carroll speaks affectionately of the little girl with "dreaming eyes of wonder" whose smile is all the payment he expects or needs for this "love gift of a fairy tale."

How far back in one's memory does this sort of wonder go? All the way to the beginning, don't you think? If you reach back for your absolutely earliest recollection of anything, chances are you will come up with some occasion where this element was very strong—that's why you remember it.

When I try to go back, I find myself looking at a small boy, three-years-old perhaps, with dark hair and greenish eyes and a thin, sunburned face. I know it is myself, but in a way it is like watching, across a great distance, another creature whose awareness of things is just beginning to come to life.

In summertime this boy lived in a tall-roofed cottage by the sea. He always felt at home in this beach house, perhaps because they were almost exactly the same age. The summer he was born, his father and mother had it built as a refuge from the relentless Georgia heat. They had brought the baby to this sandy, almost treeless coastal island when he was only a few days old, so that all his earliest impressions of saltwater sights and sounds and smells came to him there, and left him with the feeling that the house was his friend and protector and would teach him many things if he would just let it.

Of all those early impressions the sound of the sea was most pervasive, sometimes a hollow roar, sometimes a rhythmic whisper. It surrounded everything and cushioned everything and never completely went away.

Painted a dark green with white trim, the house had wide porches on three sides. From the porch that faced the ocean, wooden steps ran down to a sandy footpath leading to the beach. There pink and white oleanders gave shelter to mockingbirds and monarch butterflies, and sometimes a sinuous black snake intent on robbing nests but otherwise harmless. On the west side of the house, similar steps led to a network of boardwalks that connected the infrequent cottages and ended, half a mile away, at the terminus of the railroad that brought commuters from the city.

When I look back, two scenes seem to emerge out of the earliest mists of childhood, one involving ice and cold, the other iron and heat.

At about the same time every morning, the small boy would go and sit on the topmost of the west-facing steps. There he would wait patiently, watching the gap in the dunes where he knew the ice wagon would appear. It would come straining up the far side of the dunes, and first he would see the flicker of the mules' ears, then their grotesque heads nodding, then the silhouettes of the two figures side by side on the wooden seat, the white man driving, the black man gigantic and motionless beside him. The wheels would creak, crushing sea-oats and morning glories, throwing up plumes of sand so white and fine that it looked like sugar flung against the sky.

The boy knew that in the bed of the wagon were great cakes of ice. A ragged tarpaulin shielded them to some extent, but even so they shrank under the fierce glare of the sun, and water seeping through the floorboards left wavering stains on the sand.

As the wagon drew closer, it could be seen, astonishingly, that its occupants were conversing in sign language. Both were deaf mutes and both were called Dummy. White Dummy was a restless, sallow, hawk-faced man. At the foot of the steps he jumped down, waved to the boy, and vanished under the house where the cook, appearing from her lair in the kitchen, handed him coupons indicating how much ice was needed for the two zinc-lined ice boxes.

When White Dummy came back and flashed a sign, Black Dummy took the ice tongs, lifted a hundred-pound block as casually as if it were a pack of cigarettes, and placed it at the foot of the steps. There, using a needle-pointed ice pick, White Dummy split the block exactly in half.

The boy leaned forward, watching intently. With one more blow, White Dummy chipped off a splinter of ice about a foot long and two inches wide. He pretended to study it carefully while Black Dummy delivered the two fifty-pound blocks to the cook. Then he handed the icicle to his helper who carried it up the steps, bowed low with a sweaty grin, and presented it to the boy who stood up and bowed in return as he received it. For a moment they looked into each other's eyes. Then Black Dummy sprang like a panther back down the steps and up into the wagon. White Dummy slapped the reins. The mules lurched forward.

The boy sat down again, placing the tip of the icicle in his mouth, tasting the clear delicious coldness, feeling his hand grow numb but determined not to let go of his prize until it was melted or consumed. He watched the wagon vanish into the dunes. Today I would like to think—I know it's unreasonable—that some dim instinct in him sensed even then how remarkable for those times the silent partnership of the two icemen was. One was black, one was white, but they sat side by side. They worked as a team. They spoke their own magical language. They lived together in the house of affliction, but it pleased them to reach out through the bars and offer a small pleasure to a small boy. And this must have given him the warm and comfortable feeling that strangers were not to be feared or rejected. That friends were everywhere waiting to be made. That kindness ran like an invisible current through the universe, and so did sharing, and so did wonder.

A fragile perception, to be sure. But who can say that it didn't leave its mark?

◇———◇

The second great event of the day was the arrival, in late afternoon, of the commuter train from the city, the small steam locomotive panting after its 18-mile run across the marshes and creeks that separated the island from the mainland. When it reached the end of the line, the engine would be uncoupled and driven onto a man-powered turntable. With direction now reversed, it would steam slowly along a section of double track, past the now empty line of cars, then it would back up, recouple itself, and be ready for the return trip to the city.

For the small boy, the arrival of the train was a moment of pure magic. He knew his father would be among the commuters, limp and sodden from the city heat, with their yellowed straw hats and wrinkled seersucker suits. But even so, his whole attention was fixed on the locomotive, and especially on the tender with its bold white numerals. He could not yet read words, but he could recognize numbers. If the number was 1560, it meant that the engineer would be his friend, a wiry man with a sun-seamed face and a mouth full of gold teeth. His name was Hoops. Sometimes, if Hoops saw the boy gazing adoringly while the engine was being uncoupled, he would swing down from the cab, pick up the child in his arms, and lift him up to the black fireman who in turn deposited him on the engineer's seat.

Sitting there with the bewildering array of gauges and dials almost within reach, with the bubbling roar of the oil-fed firebox in his ears, with the hiss of steam and the smell of wisps of oil-soaked waste tucked into the pockets of Hoops' overalls, with the engineer's arms encircling him from behind, one gloved hand on the ponderous throttle, the other on the shiny brass brake, the boy felt himself transported into a realm of pure joy. Miraculously, no railroad officials appeared to protest this breach of company policy. No insurance agents wrung their hands. No apprehensive parents tried to interfere. The locomotive trembled like a leashed hound, then rolled slowly onto the turntable, where it stopped.

Stationing themselves before and behind, the fireman and a brakeman began to push on the projecting iron handles that made the turntable move. Slowly, ponderously, almost majestically, it began to swing counterclockwise, and as it did, the boy felt that the world was revolving, not the engine. The locomotive was at the center of the universe, a source of infinite power controlled and commanded by his gold-toothed friend. From the cab window the boy saw the palmettos and the oleanders and the summer cottages along the river swing past until at last, facing the other way, the locomotive was aligned once more with the track.

And now came the grandest moment of all. As the engine began to move, with a purposeful series of huffs, the boy was allowed to tug on the greasy cord that led to the great brass bell positioned halfway to the funnel and send a warning clang to anyone (there never *was* anyone) who might be dawdling or daydreaming on the tracks. They would go past the train of empty cars where the conductor, with satisfying bangs and crashes, was reversing all the seats. Past the water tank with its spout like an elephant's trunk, seldom used but always dripping and ready.

And, at last, back to the point of recoupling where the boy's custodian, perhaps his mother, perhaps some lesser member of the household, waited patiently to escort him back down the long gray boardwalk to the humdrum familiarity of home.

There, safe in bed after supper with the soothing murmur of the surf outside, he would gaze up at the tent of mosquito netting above his head and relive the wonder of the afternoon. Some day, with or without gold teeth, he too would be an engineer. He saw himself driving a locomotive of unimaginable power along gleaming rails, and a fragment of some old railroad song that Hoops had taught him pulsed inside his head:

> *Goin' to Augusta,*
> *Black an' dirty,*
> *All I need is*
> *Oil an' water,*
> *Oil an' water,*
> *Oil an' water. . . .*

Then the rhythm faded as drowsiness came down, and he carried his vision with him into the land of dreams.

◇——◇

In those days (and for many years thereafter) the boy's best friend was a middle-aged black man named Elijah Green, whose official title in the family was butler, but who also was guardian, adviser, dispenser of ancient wisdom, and enforcer of good manners where the boy was concerned. Lige never learned to read (he'd never had the chance), but everyone in the family joined in an unspoken conspiracy to keep this a secret. No one would have dreamed of embarrassing Lige by asking him to read a tide table or look up a number in the telephone book. When canned goods were bought, efforts were made to choose those with pictures on the labels so that Lige would know what to expect when he opened them.

Patient, good-humored, a fanatical consumer of Old Gold cigarettes, Lige was tolerant of everything except the household's endless succession of black cooks. When their performance failed to please him, he would mumble dreadful imprecations down the echoing shaft of the dumbwaiter. "Sickenin' " was his favorite evaluation of the unfortunate women in the kitchen below, most of whom sooner or later gave up in despair and left.

In his white coat, Lige served ten thousand meals and washed uncounted dishes. Sometimes, when the day was over, he would walk up to the village where a small group of blacks, most of them fishermen, assembled at a run-down shack known as Adam's Inn. James Adams, a six-footer who looked like a Zulu emperor, could not read or write either, but he was a marvelous fish-cleaner. If you took thirty or forty sea trout to Adam's Inn, they would always be ready in an hour, their number mysteriously reduced by three or four fish. It would have been very bad form to point out the discrepancy.

Some of James Adams' friends were seiners. In heavy wooden *bateaux*, each equipped with two sets of oars, they would row down the lazy river on a late ebb tide with their nets piled high in the stern, and set the nets where the foam-streaked waters of the ocean stretched north and south. There, off one of the blinding white beaches, they would set the seine, one man anchoring one end with feet dug into the sand, the others rowing in a vast semi-circle, spilling the net smoothly overboard so that the cork floats made a bobbing hemisphere with sinkers hugging the bottom.

When he was nine or ten years old, the boy was allowed sometimes to go with the seiners under the watchful eye of their leader, John Curry, a giant with arms and legs like tree trunks and a dead cigar always clamped between gleaming teeth. When the time came to haul in the net, a slow, backbreaking process, the boy was permitted to pull with the others, so long as he didn't get in the way. Hand over hand, inch by inch, sheer muscle power would bring in the net. Little could be seen at first, but near the end the water boiled with trapped sea creatures of every description: catfish and sting-rays, blue crabs and horseshoe crabs, copper-colored redfish, spotted seatrout and flounder, black-and-silver–striped drum, whiting that rolled their eyes (no other fish could), and croakers that protested their fate with hollow metallic grunts, while the gulls, who knew a good thing when they saw it, whirled overhead, screaming against the sky.

Sometimes the net brought in trouble. One afternoon, shouting memorable oaths, John Curry sprang into the water almost on top of a sawfish weighing at least a thousand pounds, seized it by the tail, and held on until the other fishermen could raise the net and let the sluggish intruder with its three-foot, saw-toothed bill pass harmlessly underneath. They were less lucky on another day with a nine-foot lemon shark that beat the water into a frenzy and, until it cut its way through with razor sharp teeth, dragged men and net seaward in an awesome display of power.

On that occasion, most of the catch escaped through the enormous rent in the net made by the shark, but most of the time the sea gave up its treasures peaceably, so long as poisonous catfish fins and the deadly spines on the tails of stingrays were avoided. Four or five hours of work usually netted enough edible fish to make the whole effort worthwhile. When that point was reached, John Curry would give the order to row home.

Perched high in the stern on a mound of cordage that now smelled gloriously of salt and seaweed and dead fish, the boy liked best the moment at the mouth of the river where sometimes the big rollers of the incoming tide would lift the stern of the *bateau* and propel it forward with dizzying speed while the oarsmen held their blades out of the water. It was like flying. Once, on such a run, two porpoises appeared like messengers from Neptune, one on either side of the boat, riding the same wave with effortless grace, bright eyes and smiling mouths offering a kind of aquatic friendship until at last they veered away with gasping snorts from their blowholes, a salute from one species of mammal to another.

Back at the landing, where he always thanked John Curry gravely and was given a handsome fish to take home, the boy felt as if he had been a traveler in a secret world pulsing with energy and color and life, a world so wonderful that his everyday existence seemed drab and pale by comparison.

But there was another dimension to that world now and then. When there had been a drowning along the beaches, the seiners might be called upon to recover the body. Sometimes they found it, sometimes not. On these occasions all captive fish were released, because John Curry said that otherwise the spirit of the victim would be troubled and might return. And nobody wanted that.

The boy never forgot the first time he was allowed to be a witness to one of these searches. His mother wanted to forbid it, but his father overruled her. It might be painful, he told her, but the boy should be allowed to see how unforgiving the sea could be when someone grew careless or took unnecessary chances. And so the boy watched as the body appeared—it was a young woman's—tossing and rolling as the net came in, dark hair swirling, one arm caught in the mesh of the net so that she seemed to hailing the hushed onlookers on the beach. Thus the lesson the boy's father wished him to learn was burned into his mind. And there were times on windless nights when he could almost hear the distant voices of drowned spirits who lived under the waters and whispered their warnings like far-off tolling bells: *Beware, beware, beware.*

Somewhere in the writings of the great French scientist Jacques Yves-Cousteau there is this line: "The sea, once it casts its spell, holds one in its net of wonder forever."

That is very true.

The Wonder of Growing Up

Aᔆ ᴀ ꜱᴍᴀʟʟ ʙᴏʏ, then, I found my earliest impressions conditioned by salt and sand and the silent rhythm of the tides. But there were city memories as well.

My father's home town was Savannah. My mother came from Richmond, Virginia. Each city, intensely Southern, was insulated in its own way from the mainstream of American life. Perhaps this was not a bad thing.

My mother's father, Dr. Hunter McGuire, had been Stonewall Jackson's surgeon. A bronze statue of him near the state capitol paid tribute to his skill as a physician and legendary stories about him still lingered in Richmond. Mother told me once that in the hard years just after the war her father managed to supplement his income by occasionally acting as medical attendant when hot-tempered young officers of the occupying Union forces fought duels over insults real or fancied. To watch Yankee soldiers trying to shoot one another was a privilege, my grandfather said, to be paid for it was a delight.

My Virginia grandmother still lived in a dark-paneled Victorian mansion on Grace Street where gas jets flickered and trembled inside frosted glass globes. At night these jets lighted the way upstairs. When I was a four-year-old boy this bedtime journey was an ordeal because ranged along the wall of the staircase were the heads of great antlered beasts: moose and elk and bison. Their eyes gleamed and their shadows wavered ominously in the gaslight. Some fiendish older cousins assured me that at least once every night these huge creatures jumped out of their skins, and when they did, Heaven help anyone trying to ascend the stairs. The wonder of those visits to Richmond was not proximity to my illustrious ancestors; it was my miraculous nightly escape from being devoured alive.

There were beasts in Savannah too, but these were friendly ones: two stone lions that stood guard at the entrance to my Aunt Daisy's house on Abercorn Street. They were British lions, placed there by her English father-in-law when he built the house in the 1840s, and just the right size for a four-year-old to sit upon and survey the world without fear of being eaten.

Visits to that house were a joy because Aunt Daisy, already nationally known as the founder of the Girl Scouts, was a compact, brown-eyed woman, eccentric, but warm-hearted, with an infectious laugh and enormous charm. She spoiled me shamelessly, partly because, being quite deaf herself, she sympathized with the periodic ear infections that caused me much misery. I could always count on her coming to my aid when necessary. Once, I remember, when a visitor asked me what I intended to be when I grew up, I sat silent and embarrassed, but Aunt Daisy spoke up cheerily. "I'll tell you what he's going to be," she said. "He's going to be astonished!" I think she was talking about the gift of wonder. She certainly had it, and hoped I'd have it too.

Aunt Daisy was a great animal lover. At one point, she had a pet mockingbird that sat on her shoulder and nibbled at her pen as she wrote letters. And countless dogs. She also had a malevolent blue-and-yellow macaw named Polly Poons, who would bite you with little or no provocation, and also made guttural comments on the human race from time to time that were a source of fascination and wonder.

Once Aunt Daisy gave me a strong-willed Shetland pony named Buster Brown. If Buster Brown did not get his way when you were riding him, he would rear up and fall on his back. You had to be able to jump off in a hurry. He also had a tendency to shy violently at a falling leaf or a scrap of newspaper, or sometimes at nothing at all. When I complained to Aunt Daisy, she assured me solemnly that horses and ponies see everything eight times its normal size, so naturally to them a windblown newspaper was eight times as frightening as it would be to a human. This struck me as a reasonable explanation, and I forgave Buster Brown everything—which, of course, was exactly what Aunt Daisy intended.

Sometimes, when our parents would escape during the summer for a few weeks of vacation, Aunt Daisy would come down to the beach cottage and take charge of everything. This often led to strange and marvelous adventures. If I took Aunt Daisy fishing in my little rowboat, for instance, she would wrap herself in so many veils (to fend off mosquitoes, though there really were none) that she looked like some kind of visiting Arab. She also brought along a mallet which I was to use to rap on the head any fish we caught, "to keep it from suffering." All this brought me a dubious notoriety among my friends on the river, but it did not diminish my affection for Aunt Daisy.

In those days at the beach there were few diversions—no movies, no church of our denomination—and so sometimes on Sunday nights we would sit around and sing hymns. There was nothing very pious about this, we just liked to sing. Each of us four children was allowed to choose a favorite, and if we had young house guests, they were supposed to participate too. If they did not know a hymn, we would assign them one, usually *Onward, Christian Soldiers,* the theory being that only barbarians would fail to know that one.

The hymn I always chose was an old Moody & Sankey offering called *Pull For the Shore.* It had a robust tune and told the story of some shipwrecked sailor trying to escape in a lifeboat from his sinking vessel; he was exhorted to "leave the poor old stranded wreck and pull for the shore." I liked this one partly because it had a strong nautical flavor, and partly because there was a family legend connected to it. In the legend, some ne'er-do-well cousin had a hopeless drinking problem that grew worse and worse until one night, as he sat stupefied over his drink in some seedy tavern, a great light suddenly seemed to shine down upon him and a mighty voice sounded in his ears: "Leave the poor old stranded wreck!" Recognizing himself instantly in this description, he got up, left his drink on the bar, staggered out, and never touched liquor again.

Once I asked Father if the story was true. "I never looked for proof," said Father. "Unverified stories are often the best."

So I settled for that.

Mother used to listen to the Sunday evening songfests with an indulgent smile. She had a good voice herself, but I think something in her Richmond background held a more formal view of religion. Perhaps she found our boisterous music a bit undignified. Anyway, she never joined in, but sat relaxed in the yellow lamplight, a truly beautiful woman—everyone said so—with splendid gray eyes and dark hair piled on top of her head. She and my father had a pet name for each other—"Wabes." We children never knew where the name came from or what it meant. But it obviously meant a lot to them.

Most of the time Mother was serene and soft-spoken, but when something made her angry, everyone knew it. One Sunday afternoon, while we were sitting on the porch after two-o'clock dinner, anguished cries for help came from the ocean where at certain tides, there was a deep channel between sandbars and a fierce current. These crises happened at least twice every summer. Father ran down the steps and onto the beach with the rest of us close behind. He kicked off his shoes, handed his wallet to someone in the small crowd of onlookers that had gathered, plunged into the water fully clothed, and finally pulled the flailing victim back to land. Then, when he asked for his wallet, no one seemed to have it.

Mother turned on the spectators like a tigress. If that wallet was not placed in her hands within ten seconds, she said in a quietly deadly voice, the police would be summoned, and if not the police, the military authorities at Fort Screven, the battery of coastal defense guns a few miles down the beach. Everyone would be searched. No one would be permitted to leave the island. There was a stunned silence. Finally a sheepish individual handed over the wallet, mumbling implausible excuses about having "forgotten" it. I remember thinking that Mother's threat about the military was not an entirely empty one. The commander of the garrison at Screven was a friend who sometimes came to dinner. I think he really would have sent a squad of military police if Mother had asked him. His name: Col. George C. Marshall. The world would hear a good deal about him twenty years or so down the road.

The summer days slipped by like beads on a golden chain, but the time always came when we had to go back to town, put on shoes and grimly return to school. The school was a private one that had been founded by Miss Nina Pape, a well-trained educator, who was a close friend of Aunt Daisy. Indeed, she was the one who received the memorable telephone call on the evening of Daisy's return from England in 1912 that marked the birth of Girl Scouting in America. "Nina, come right over. I've got something for the girls of Savannah and the whole country and the whole world, and we're going to start it tonight!"

Miss Pape, tall and angular, always wore black with a black ribbon at her throat. She walked with an ungainly stride that made her look like a tottering lighthouse. Where she recruited her teachers, no one quite knew, but they were a colorful lot.

There was Madame Labouchère, a French widow from Alsace-Lorraine, who was said to have been badly shellshocked during the war. She wore an enormous wig into which she absent-mindedly thrust pencils as the day wore on, until by day's end she resembled an agitated porcupine. Madame Labouchère could not stand loud noises. If we tramped by her classroom on the un-carpeted floor, she would come flying out at us, shrieking, *"Doucement! Doucement!"* We would mock her gleefully, "Do some more!" And proceed to do it.

We would never have dared take such liberties with our Latin teacher, Miss Emily Charlton, into whose class I stumbled at the age of twelve or thirteen. Miss Charlton refused to admit that what she had on her hands was a shiftless and no-account col-lection of giggly and grubby teen-agers. She was going to drive Latin into our heads if it killed us, and it very nearly did.

Mistakes were not tolerated in Miss Charlton's class. You did your homework, because if you didn't, Miss Charlton would make you stand up. Then she would point at you with an accus-ing finger backed by glittering black eyes. "Pure, unadulterated, inexcusable carelessness!" she would say. You wished the floor would open up and swallow you.

Truth was, Miss Charlton did not just teach Latin. She also taught standards—how to set them, how to meet them, how to feel a thrill of satisfaction when they were met. She was a glori-ous and unassailable high priestess of knowledge. She demanded the best, she insisted on the best, and she got it, too. When I took my entrance examinations to a big northern prep school, my grades in French and algebra were dismal, but I got a 99 in Latin. Totally unlike Miss Charlton was a dreamy young man who taught English. He was named Mr. Twombly. He gave everyone good grades whether they earned them or not, but he also regarded words with awe and wonder, and did his best to make that wonder rub off on us.

One February morning, Mr. Twombly decided to read the Gettysburg Address aloud. He knew that most of us in that Georgia classroom were descendants of Confederate soldiers, and he conceded that Abraham Lincoln was undeniably a Yankee. But, said Mr. Twombly, he was the greatest of Yankees and deserved universal respect, even from the likes of us.

So he read the Address. "Four-score and seven years ago," he began. We listened indifferently because most of us had heard it before.

When he finished, Mr. Twombly came around his desk and sat on the edge of it, facing us. "On that November day in 1863," he said, "there were in the audience many widows and grieving parents of the men who had died there only a few months earlier. Many Confederate soldiers, equally brave, had fallen also. The greatest values on both sides—love of home, love of country— were not so very different. Perhaps some day you may be called upon to defend those same values. I hope not, but we all know that it's possible."

Mr. Twombly moved over to the blackboard, picked up a piece of chalk, and wrote three words. "Near the end, Lincoln uses these words. They have tremendous power. If you listen carefully, you can hear the ring of steel in them. To make sure that you never forget them, I'm going to read the last few lines. When I pause and raise my finger, I want you to whisper these three words together, then louder when I raise two fingers and loudest of all when I raise three fingers. Are you ready?"

We all nodded. Mr. Twombly cleared his throat and read in a slow, steady voice: "We here highly resolve that these dead shall not have died in vain—that this nation, under God, shall have a new birth of freedom—and that government of the people, by the people, for the people. . . ." He stopped reading and held up one finger.

". . . shall not perish . . ." we murmured in unison.

Mr. Twombly raised a second finger. "Shall not perish!" we chanted louder.

He raised a third finger. "SHALL NOT PERISH!" we shouted.

Mr. Twombly smiled, closed the book, and gave us Lincoln's final words. ". . . from the earth," he said.

◇——◇

Who can say when childhood ends? Is it a gradual thing, or is there perhaps a single moment that more often than not passes unrecognized?

A few pages back we left a very small boy drowsing under a mosquito net, dreaming grand dreams of becoming a locomotive engineer. But he could not stay there, and his dreams could not stay there either. The years went by, slowly at first, then more and more swiftly. He grew taller and stronger, but still some essential part of him lingered in the sunglow of childhood.

By the time they were in their teens, the boy and most of his friends were skilled bodysurfers. Of all his contacts with saltwater, this was the most intimate and the most exciting. When a great wave seizes you and flings you shoreward, you are no longer merely in the ocean, you are a part of it. There were no surfboards in those days, just the swimmer and the pounding pulse of the sea, sometimes friendly, and sometimes not.

The best waves of all were the giant glassy rollers that came speeding westward from a hurricane or tropical storm passing by a hundred miles or so offshore. They wasted no power until they were ready to break, but then you might find yourself on top of a precipice staring down into a seething, mist-filled chasm so deep and menacing that you might lose your nerve and back off, because if you plunged too soon and let the wave break on top of you, it might hammer you to the bottom and hold you there until your lungs screamed for air and you thought you might never see the sky again. It was an endless thrill, an endless challenge, an endless wonder.

Once, when he was about sixteen, the lure of the surf proved too much for the boy. He had spent most of his summer days working on a shrimp boat and some of his evenings in the company of a sweet-tempered girl whose chief ambition in life seemed to be to teach him how to dance. When the time came for him to return to his New England preparatory school, he bade the girl a fond farewell and took the train to New York. He intended to stop over and visit a schoolmate on Long Island for three or four days before classes began. But when he arrived at Pennsylvania Station, a newspaper headline informed him that a small hurricane moving up from Florida was expected to pass by the coastal islands of Georgia in the next few hours. He hesitated just for a moment, and then spent most of his summer's earnings on an additional round trip ticket that would take him back over the eight hundred miles he had just traveled. He felt a bit uneasy about his father's reaction to this lunacy, but he decided to risk it.

Arriving early at the beach house, he found his father at breakfast, barricaded as usual behind the morning newspaper. The boy could not see his face. He sat down anyway, and there was silence for a while.

Finally his father said, "This is an unexpected pleasure."

"I know," the boy said sheepishly.

Another silence. Then, "Tell me," said his father, "what was the irresistible attraction that lured you back? Was it a happy home? Or a pretty girl? Or just the prospect of large waves?"

"Very large waves," the boy murmured.

His father lowered the newspaper. "I suppose you think I'm angry with you. Actually I'm glad there's a little harmless foolishness in you. I never had time for much when I was your age." He pushed back his chair and stared out the window where the early sunlight gilded the beach and an enormous sea rolled green and gold. "So when you get out there, which I know you're dying to do, ride a couple of big ones for me, will you?" He put down the newspaper. "And now, if you'll excuse me, I have to go and catch my train."

The boy followed his father to the door and watched as the slender, familiar figure walked down the boardwalk to join the other commuters hurrying toward the train. As he did, an unaccustomed idea brushed across the surface of his mind, the thought that it was not just a parent, not just a symbol of authority moving away from him. It was also a friend. Then the siren call of the surf sounded again in his ears, and he went to answer it.

But he was a child no longer.

The Invisible Stream

OVER THE YEARS in all my reading whenever I came upon the word *epiphany*, I was never quite sure what it meant. Something mysterious and grand, no doubt. But what? I was too lazy to look it up, so I would skip over it or hurry past it, feeling faintly guilty because I am supposed to be knowledgeable about words.

The other day the guilt finally drove me to the dictionary. There, among the definitions of epiphany, I found this one: "an intuitive grasp of reality through something usually simple and striking."

Well, now that I more or less knew the meaning of epiphany,

I found myself wondering if such sudden intuitions had ever occurred in my own life. And memory took me back all the way to college days before I found one that might qualify.

The college I chose so long ago was a famous one with very good teachers, dedicated men who did their best to propel us along the thorny road that led to more than mere competence in whatever discipline they were teaching. I have to admit, though, that sometimes I felt I learned more on the playing field than in the classroom.

One sport I learned a lot from was rowing. On the surface, crew racing looks like a somewhat mindless demonstration of youthful strength and not much more. But there is more. Anyone who ever has been part of an eight-oared crew will tell you that it may well be the most demanding of sports. It stretches your endurance to the absolute bone-cracking limit. It requires exquisite timing from eight individuals. There are no stars or prima-donnas in a racing shell. Everyone is equal. It calls for complete coordination, physical and mental, from everyone in the boat.

This coordination comes only from practice. The more miles a crew rows together, the closer it comes to the complete unity, the absolute oneness that it is always seeking. And can never quite attain.

Most practice sessions are routine, but I remember one in my junior year that was not. Years later I tried to describe what made it different, but I had no name for it then. Now I think I do.

It was early spring on the Housatonic, Connecticut's loveliest river; the trees were just beginning to show feathers of green. We had rowed several miles upstream from the boathouse on an ordinary practice run, trailed as usual by the white coaching launch. It was one of those days when nothing seemed to please the hooded figure with the megaphone in the bow of the launch. Sarcasm was the lash our coach sometimes used to sting us into better performance. On this day he apparently judged our performance too dismal to merit any comment at all. Finally, miles from home, he announced that he could not bear to look at us any longer, whereupon he turned the launch around and sped downstream, leaving us there.

It was a surly crew that started the long row back. You could almost hear the mutinous thoughts running through every head. *So we aren't so good. So what? So who cares about this crazy sport anyway? Only an idiot would choose to spend his time this way.* And so on.

By now it was almost dark. The trees were massed shadows along the tranquil river; the sunset had faded; the first stars were beginning to show through. We slogged along morosely at about twenty-two strokes per minute, far below racing speed. The shell felt heavy, lifeless; every stroke was an effort.

Then an extraordinary thing happened. As if a master conductor was orchestrating it, the ragged timing became flawless. The friction of the water vanished; the shell seemed to skim along on quicksilver. The pressure on the oar blades seemed to disappear; they were like feathers drawing long smooth lines through empty air. Everything was effortless—no strain, no stress, just perfect rhythm, pure exhilaration, astonished joy. There was no sound except the hiss of water under the shell, and the muffled double thump of eight oars striking the river at precisely the same split second and releasing it again with the same marvelous precision. It was not like rowing; it was like flying. And all of us knew it.

How long it lasted I do not know. Perhaps half a mile, maybe a mile. Then it began to fade. By the time we reached the boathouse, it was gone.

Would it be fair to say that those five minutes on the shadowed Housatonic involved some kind of epiphany? If so, what was the "intuitive grasp of reality" being offered? Was it that if you do something really right, the struggle to do it disappears? Was it that when you do, there is no fatigue, no strain, no effort at all because you are in harmony with something that simply brushes those things aside?

I have always believed that there are great unseen rhythms and patterns that underlie all reality. Is it conceivable that among those rhythms is a mighty current of perfection, running like a stream or river on the borders of our lives, beyond our reach almost all the time but sometimes allowing us to come close to it?

When that happens, it is an epiphany, I suppose. But there is another word that I like better—*wonder*.

A Place of Dreaming Spires

SOMETIMES I THINK there are two kinds of wonder. One is the sudden and unexpected kind that comes at you like a flash of lightning. I would say my encounter with the spider web belonged in that category. Then there is a quiet kind of wonder, more sustained, more a glow than a flash, that can surround a special place for a certain period of time. Both kinds are to be sought. Both are to be treasured.

Centuries ago in England, at a place where a river was shallow enough for oxen to cross, a town grew up known as Oxenford, or Oxford. In the Middle Ages, colleges clustered there and finally a university was named after the town itself. "That sweet city," Matthew Arnold called it, "with its dreaming spires."

In my early twenties, thanks to a scholarship, I went to Oxford for a couple of years. I am afraid I was motivated, not so much by an unquenchable thirst for knowledge, as by my fear of the Great Depression. I wanted to put off plunging into those chilly waters as long as possible. And I was lucky in my timing. In history, as in human lives, some periods are more wonder-filled than others. Between the two World Wars, Oxford was a place where a golden light of tranquility and harmony seemed to pervade everything.

Everything conspired to make life pleasant. Studies were not very demanding. Holidays came around frequently. If you could afford to travel around Britain or on the continent, fine. If not, a remarkable woman named Lady Frances Ryder, who seemed to know everyone in England, would arrange for you to be invited to country homes, where the owners were happy to have foreign students as guests. You could tell Lady Frances what your favorite activities were, and she would send you to a host family that could offer them: golf, tennis, horseback riding, fishing, shooting, bridge, whatever. Sometimes there were unmarried young ladies of the household who would regard you with interested eyes. If you behaved reasonably well, you were almost certain to be asked back. The hospitality of those people was astonishing. They provided everything and expected nothing in return.

When the colleges were in session, life was studded with magical moments. Not just lectures and concerts, campuses everywhere have those. No, it was the simple and easy going things you could do almost any time, and come to take for granted if you didn't watch out. You could borrow a car and visit Stratford or Stonehenge. You could spend a rainy afternoon browsing in one of the world's oldest libraries, or row with an eight-oared crew. You could ride your bicycle a mile or two up the Thames and drink brown ale in an inn that dated back to the eleventh century. You could sit on an emerald lawn and eat strawberries and watch a twilight performance of *A Midsummer Night's Dream.* At dawn on the first day of May, you could climb to the top of a tower that was old when the Pilgrims sailed, and hear robed choirboys sing a Latin hymn to May Day, and watch costumed folk dancers on the bridge below.

No doubt we met minor problems or disappointments now and then, but most of the time we seemed to be living in a universe wondrously arranged for the maximum contentment of a handful of privileged young people, namely, us.

Two of my best friends at Oxford were a girl named Mary from Vancouver and a boy named Hugh from Oklahoma. The three of us used to travel together on the continent during some of the vacations. We had little money, so we traveled by bus, stayed in hostels and cheap pensions, visited endless churches and museums where admission was free, sat in sidewalk cafes, tried to master the local language, laughed a lot, and worried about nothing.

Sometimes—wonder of wonders—we even learned something about life. There was the time in Spain when we stayed with a family that took in paying guests. The place was comfortable enough, but strangely sombre. The owner, whose name was Linares, never smiled. His wife—we called her La Señora—always wore black. There was a grand piano in the living room, but it was always closed. A maid told us that La Señora had been a concert pianist, but two years earlier her son had been killed in a car crash. She had not touched the piano since.

This part of Spain was sherry country, and we discovered that most wine-cellars—*bodegas,* they were called—would offer a sample glass or two to visitors who showed interest in their product. Therefore, if you went from one *bodega* to another, the cares of the world had a tendency to fade away.

One afternoon, having spent some time in this fashion, the three of us came back to the Linares house in a very good humor indeed. Without thinking, Hugh sat down at the piano and began to play some popular song, rather badly, while Mary and I sang along enthusiastically. We did make quite a lot of noise.

Suddenly a door opened and the maid rushed in, wringing her hands. Behind her came Linares, looking stricken, urging us with gestures to desist. At the same time another door opened and there stood La Señora, tall and tragic in her mourning clothes. The music died. We were terribly embarrassed. No one knew what to say or do. Then La Señora smiled. She came forward, pushed Hugh aside, and began to play the triumphal march from *Aida.* Great crashing chords seemed to fill the whole house, driving the shadows away. I remember how the little maid crossed herself, how Linares burst into tears. It was a moment of pure wonder, and though we did not fully comprehend it then, later we understood. La Señora had felt concern, not for herself, but for us. And her compassion had driven her grief away.

Each spring at Oxford, there was a six-day period that had a flavor all its own. This was Eights Week, when the eight-oared crews belonging to the various colleges competed and spectators came from towns as far away as London to cheer for their favorites.

For oarsmen like myself, trained in America, rowing at Oxford was a unique experience. The river was so narrow that crews could not race abreast. They had to compete in single file, the objective for each crew being to bump—literally—the one ahead before the one behind could do the same to it. When a bump was scored, both crews had to pull out of the race. The next day they exchanged starting positions. Thus, in an endless quest to become "Head of the River," a crew could move up several places during Eights Week or, conversely, could fall back. On the towpath, only a few yards away from the straining crews, a horde of coaches and well-wishers rushed along, shouting encouragement, bawling advice through megaphones, sometimes firing pistols with blank cartridges to signal when a bump was possible or imminent. Wild and glorious madness! On the far side of the river, a series of gaily painted barges—each college had one—served as spectator points and as dressing rooms for the crews. The whole scene had a marvelous kind of visual wonderment.

Also during Eights Week, it was customary for the famed D'Oyly Carte theatrical company from London to present Gilbert & Sullivan operettas, a different one each night. Admission prices were very low. Student audiences were enthusiastic. We learned all the music and most of the words.

Another wonder of Oxford was the Bach Choir. Hugh and Mary were members and persuaded me to join. I don't know why they let me in. My ability to read music was limited and I survived mainly by imitating the other singers. But when four hundred voices began rolling through one of Bach's motets or Handel's *Messiah,* the enormous rhythm and power reminded me somehow of the steam locomotives I had admired so extravagantly as a small boy.

I remember coming out of a rehearsal one night into the fading twilight, still singing, Mary's clear soprano soaring up over the shadowy towers and darkened streets: "... and His Name shall be called: Wonderful, Counsellor, The Mighty God, The Everlasting Father, The Prince of Peace!"

The last of the sunset lingered in the west, but to the east blueblack clouds of a massive thunderstorm were advancing on the city. It was just as well that none of us could see into the future.

The Battle of Britain was less than four years away.

War Memories

I COME FROM a long line of soldiers, but I never expected to be one. When I thought about it at all, I told myself that I was not good military material. I was too resistant to authority, for one thing. Probably not brave enough either, if it came to facing real danger.

But then the Nazis seized power in Germany and overran Europe. The Japanese made their strike at Pearl Harbor. Suddenly we were in it. And those of us who chose voluntarily to join the armed services found ourselves at the mercy of enormous unseen forces that determined where we went, how we served, and ultimately, whether we lived or died. The sense of control and purpose that had been ours in civilian life vanished. What happened now depended simply on the next throw of the iron dice of war.

Was there anything that could be called wonderful about this?

Two things, maybe. One was the astonishing closeness that sprang up between total strangers who found themselves in the same military unit, facing the same uncertainties and hazards. The other was a heightened sense of aliveness and awareness. The dust of daily routine was blown away. Things had a new intensity, a new reality. Sometimes you liked that reality, sometimes not.

The Eighth Air Force was just starting operations in England. They needed Squadron Intelligence Officers, known as S-2s, preferably with some experience in Britain. So a handful of us were selected and sent overseas late in 1942.

In England only four groups of heavy bombers were operating at the time. They were suffering heavy casualties and replacements were slow. The S-2s lived very close to the combat crews and sometimes became deeply involved with them emotionally. When a bomber failed to return from a mission, it was like having a death in the family.

Everyone who has lived through a war has memories, some good, some bad, some exciting, some painful. When I sift through my own, there are two that seem to have the luminous quality of wonder that I have been trying to recapture.

The setting for the first was a bomber base in East Anglia. Most of our bases were nothing but concrete runways and Nissen huts and mud, but before the war this one had been a permanent RAF base. It was built around a tiny English village, complete with a manor house and a little church. There were quaint thatched houses for married officers, and there was more grass than mud, and the mess hall even had curtains in the windows.

The target that day was Brunswick, and some of us intelligence officers were on the control tower when the sun came up, watching the planes take off. I remember how behind the whirling discs of the propellers moisture trails hung in the new-washed air. And when the prop blasts flattened the wheat growing along the runways, you could see the crimson fire of poppies showing below the green.

At about nine o'clock, I decided to walk back to the briefing room. It was the most beautiful winter day I had ever seen in England. There was not a cloud, the air seemed almost warm, and there was this unbelievable sunshine gilding everything—the Nissen huts and the narrow roads and the old manor house and the little church.

There were more bombers in the sky then than you would have thought possible. One combat wing was coming over right behind another, about sixty Fortresses in each wing, all stacked up precise and proud. Somehow they looked more serene than menacing against that gentle sky, but their engines created a canopy of sound that was almost terrifying. I walked along with my head in the air and when I got to the church the organ began to play for the morning service. The tones were curiously loud and sweet for such a little church. They seemed so indifferent to the thunder of the bombers that it gave me a strange feeling. And just then a girl came around the corner.

She was tall and she walked with a long, swinging stride, and even at a distance there was something very colorful and very feminine about her. She had on some kind of bright scarf and a tweed skirt and yellow worsted stockings. You know she must have been striking to get away with that, and she did. She came straight down the middle of the road carrying a little suitcase. I figured she had come up from London for the station dance that night. Later I learned that her name was Pamela, but just then she needed no name. As she came closer, I could see that she had a soft, scarlet mouth—they wore a lot of lipstick in those days— and a great mane of shining blond hair, the kind you'd like to crush in your hands. I could see some bicycle riders waver a little and whistle at her as she passed by, and some joker stuck his head out of a mess hall window and made the motion of grinding an imaginary movie camera.

The bombers kept streaming over the church tower, and the organ kept sounding its deep defiant chords, and the girl kept coming closer, and the whole moment had a vividness, a timelessness, a kind of wonder that I knew with certainty would never fade.

And it hasn't because in the end, you see, I married that girl.

◇———◇

The war seemed to go on forever, but I can pinpoint the exact moment when it ended for me and for millions of others in the British Isles. Germany had been collapsing for many weeks; we knew the surrender was coming. It was just a question of which day, and finally we even knew that.

I was somewhere in Germany, but I wanted very much to be in Britain with Pam when the lights came on again. By now I was pretty good at hitching rides on military aircraft, so I flew to Paris and then on to London.

It was late afternoon when I got there; the long soft summer twilight was just beginning. Some English friends told Pam and me that as darkness fell the King and Queen would be making an appearance on the balcony at Buckingham Palace.

So we went down and joined the vast crowd that was waiting outside the palace. Every kind of person seemed to be there—office workers, lorry drivers, hospital attendants, soldiers and sailors in the uniforms of a dozen nations—all watching the empty balcony draped with a crimson banner embroidered in gold with the royal initials. No one said anything. The faces were grave and patient and expectant. As we stood there, dusk seemed to eddy from the ground, but the western sky still held streaks of saffron, and through this afterglow a flight of mallard ducks kept circling the dark mass of the palace, almost as if they too were waiting for something.

As the minutes passed, a whole cavalcade of wartime recollections came streaming across my mind. I remembered walking alone through the London blackout with air raid sirens sounding the all-clear and searchlights quartering the blue-black vault of midnight; it was like being inside an enormous star-sapphire. I remembered the frustrating days in an Army hospital after a parachute jump left me with a broken leg. I remembered the morning the buzz bomb blew in all the windows of our flat; the sound of the explosion was like having a gigantic whip cracked inside your skull. But we were unharmed.

At last a spotlight cut through the darkness, and the King and Queen and the two little princesses came out on the balcony and smiled and waved. A great roar went up from the crowd that had been so silent. At this precise moment, at least for us, the war in Europe ended and all of us knew it. In that roar was all the affection and respect that these unconquerable people felt for the slender man on the balcony who had stayed with them through all the hardships, all the setbacks, all the disasters and was still with them at this moment of victory. He was the symbol of it all, in their tribute to him there was something tremendous and good and true.

This feeling of exaltation stayed with us as the crowd went streaming away through London's streets, where the dusty blackout curtains were being pulled aside and the unaccustomed lights were beginning to glow and drinks could be had almost anywhere for little money or none at all. There was dancing in the streets, and we saw a young British sailor climb the boarded-up statue of Eros in Piccadilly Circus and fasten a Union Jack to the top of it. I kept remembering all the crises these people had passed through with never a whimper, never a thought of surrender. I was just an American from far away, and I knew we Americans had been slow in coming to help them, but we were here now and we had helped them, and I knew they would not mind sharing the wonder of their triumph with us.

There was more than enough to go around.

Ideas:
The Key to
Everything

The world will never starve for wonders; but
only for want of wonder.

G.K. Chesterton

S O THE WAR CAME to an end, and with a sigh of considerable relief most of us went home, took off our uniforms, and settled down to the task of making a living, or raising a family, or both.

For the next few years I swung back and forth between magazine editing and free-lance writing. They were opposite sides of the same coin, really. A successful editor must have some writing skills. A successful writer must have some capacity to edit his own work. Of the two occupations, I think editing is easier and, if you like people, more fun. An editor is constantly in touch with all sorts of colorful characters. Writers have to be more solitary. Editors have other people's literary problems thrust at them. Writers have to invent their own problems before they can begin to solve them.

Whether you choose to be editor or writer, one commodity is in constant demand: ideas. A magazine is nothing but a collection of ideas assembled by editors into a single package. Before a writer can attempt an article or a short story or a novel, he must have a valid idea. Ideas are the key to everything.

Where do ideas come from? Sometimes, apparently out of nowhere. In the days when I wrote a good deal of magazine fiction, occasionally a story would jump into my head, fully formed, complete with plot and characters and dialogue, waiting to be set down on paper. A psychiatrist would have said, no doubt, that it was born and developed in my unconscious mind. Maybe so. It was a welcome wonder when it happened.

When I was wearing my editor's hat, I tried very hard to identify with my readers. What were they looking for? How could I supply it? I knew they wanted to be entertained, but there was more to it than that. They also wanted to be helped, to be encouraged, to be shown how to improve themselves mentally and physically and spiritually. They wanted to be provided with armor and weapons for the struggle of life. When you were able to supply these things, your reward was an inner glow that made all the effort worth while.

Sometimes an editor will hand a writer—lucky writer!—a good idea. Once DeWitt Wallace, founder and editor of *Reader's Digest,* said to me, "Why don't you try an article called 'The Engaging Art of Laughing at Yourself'?" What a simple, bright, original idea! That was an easy one to attempt, because if Mr. Wallace wanted it, selling it would not be difficult.

When I was wearing my writer's cap, I used to listen for helpful words or phrases, usually spoken by older or wiser friends, that I could relay to readers without sounding too preachy or pompous myself. Such literary larceny never bothered me. For one thing, I was always careful to credit the source. For another, I guess I saw myself (ah, rationalization!) as a kind of literary Robin Hood, stealing helpful ideas from people who had them in order to bring them to people who did not.

Sometimes it was not the ideas themselves that attracted me so much as the way they were expressed, the manner in which the words were arranged. Some of these memories go all the way back to my childhood. Here are a few.

MISS LUCY, INVERTED

When we were youngsters growing up in our sleepy Southern town, most of the parents and grandparents of my friends seemed rather staid and sober folk, not very exciting. But there was one memorable exception: Miss Lucy. Miss Lucy was a widow lady in her sixties, or thereabouts, who lived with her sister Clara. Clara was prim and proper, but Miss Lucy was full of charm and sparkle and enthusiasm.

One day in the course of assuring some of us that age need not be a barrier to anything, Miss Lucy asserted that she could still stand on her head whenever she felt like it. When we looked doubtful, she proceeded to do so, clamping her skirt between her knees and beaming at us upside down.

"Oh, Lucy," said Clara disapprovingly. "Do be your age!"

Miss Lucy righted herself and looked at her sister. "Be your age?" she said. "What sort of nonsense is that? How can anyone be anything *but* their age? The trick is to *love* your age, whatever it is. Love it when you're young and strong and foolish. Love it when you're old and wise. Love it in the middle when the challenges come and you can fly at them and solve some of them, maybe most of them. If you love your age, you'll never go around wishing you were some other age. Think about that now and then, Clara. Might do you good!"

I don't know whether Miss Lucy's words had any effect on her sister. I do know they did on me. They were spoken more than fifty years ago. But I remember them still.

GLENN, ON GIVING

Does it bother you when a beggar or a panhandler approaches you on the street? It does me. It's not that I am afraid of the panhandler, although I suppose nowadays some of them can be dangerous. Rather, I'm uneasy about my own reactions and responses. What should they be?

I was walking to work one day in New York with Glenn Kittler, a warm and wonderful man who lived in an uptown apartment with a cat named Louie. As we came to a corner we were approached by a faded woman, poorly dressed, who told us pitifully that she needed money because her children were hungry. Glenn pulled out a handful of change and gave it to her.

As we moved on, I said disapprovingly, "That woman's here every day with that same story. She'll probably just buy a drink with the money you gave her."

"Perhaps she will," Glenn said. "But you know, I think God sometimes sends people like that just to test our charity." We walked a little farther, then he said quietly, almost to himself, "The act of giving is more important than the merit of the receiver."

There are times when I need to remember that.

FATHER, ON HAPPINESS

Father was a man who loved words and enjoyed finding new meanings in them. One Fourth of July he was talking about that famous phrase from the Declaration of Independence—life, liberty and the pursuit of happiness.

"I suppose we all do chase after happiness," Father said. "But sometimes I wonder if it isn't the other way 'round. Maybe happiness is pursuing us. And if it never catches up, it may be because something is wrong in the way we're living our lives."

He went on to say that we live in a universe of mighty laws, physical and spiritual, and that by and large a person is happy in proportion as he or she is in harmony with those laws.

"This means that if you want happiness to overtake you," Father said, "you have to try to get rid of selfishness and dishonesty and anger and guilt and all the other roadblocks that keep it from catching up. When you clear those things out of your life and keep them out, you're giving happiness a chance to come right up and tap you on the shoulder."

Is happiness catching up with us? Is it falling behind? Something to think about now and then, I do believe.

BARBARA, ON OPTIONS

I know a woman who is badly crippled by arthritis. Barbara's hands are almost useless, and she is in constant pain. And yet she is always cheerful and uncomplaining.

Not long ago I tried to tell her how much I admired her. "If I had to endure the limitations and suffering you face every day," I said, "I'd be miserable."

She smiled a little. "I'll quote you something I read somewhere: 'Pain is inevitable. Misery is optional.' I forget who said it, but it packs a lot into just six words, don't you think?"

She went on to say that physical pain is a fact that comes with living, just as illness or financial woes or broken relationships are facts. But misery is a state of mind, a reaction to the facts, that can be controlled or altered by an act of will.

"There really is an option," Barbara said. "You can choose to dwell upon your troubles, or not. You can choose to be filled with gloom and despair, or you can bar the door to them."

"Not always an easy choice," I said.

"No, it's not," my friend agreed. "But I've developed a simple technique that seems to work for me. If I find myself beginning to feel sorry for myself, or discouraged, or depressed, I open the doors and windows of my mind and invite those unwelcome visitors to leave. Then I ask the Lord to fill the spaces left by the hobgoblins with His peace and light and love. And He does."

Now, whenever I am feeling low, I try to remember what my friend said: "Misery is optional." Hobgoblins, begone!

The Bricklayer

All churches have something to say to a visitor, I think, if they will just stand still and listen. The other day I found myself in the First African Baptist Church in my hometown, Savannah. It stands facing Franklin Square, gaunt and angular, with a certain power that is hard to explain unless you know something about its history.

It was built by slaves at the beginning of the Civil War. Their owners allowed them to work on it at night by the light of bonfires after their other tasks were done. Many were illiterate, but some were also skilled carpenters and masons. The women brought bricks in their aprons to the men as they worked. Records of the construction are almost nonexistent except for a single phrase in an old ledger: "The man who laid the first brick was the man who laid the last."

How could people held in bondage and denied education build a brick edifice capable of seating more than a thousand worshipers? The answer is that someone must have led them, one of their own number, someone who laid the first brick with faith and hope and determination, and then four years later laid the last.

Today, no one knows who that leader was, but the church is his monument and his glory.

More often than I like to acknowledge, I become discouraged in the middle of a project. Sometimes I give up altogether. But now I think I have a phrase to remember when that temptation comes, when it is much easier to stop than go on. *The man who laid the first brick laid the last.*

Dr. Karl, On Life's Purpose

Someone asked me once which of the many people that I have interviewed over the years had impressed me most. Not an easy question, but I found my mind going back to a visit I made to the Menninger Foundation in Topeka, Kansas, and the time I spent with Dr. Karl Menninger, considered the dean of American psychiatrists. I felt then that I was in the presence of a towering genius, and nothing since has caused me to change my mind.

I can recall his office very vividly—the Navaho rugs on the floor, the Native American artifacts everywhere, Dr. Karl wearing a yellow shirt with turquoise cufflinks, peering at me with eyes that were both penetrating and kind.

We were talking about the importance of hope in human affairs. "If you lose all hope," the doctor said, "you stop trying and you stop caring. That won't do. I think each of us is put here to dilute the misery in the world. You may not be able to make a big contribution, but you can make a little one, and you've got to try."

Help dilute the misery in the world. A tremendous challenge, and an uncompromising yardstick. It might profit all of us to think about it at bedtime once in a while. Ask yourself honestly which of your actions during the day came close to fitting that definition. If you can think of a few, sleep soundly.

If not, don't despair. The sun will rise again tomorrow. You'll have plenty of opportunities then.

Those Little Black Marks

OUR LONG-AGO ENGLISH TEACHER, Mr. Twombly, was right. There is great power in words. And great mystery. And endless marvels. Rudyard Kipling paid tribute to their importance in his life and work:

> *I keep six honest serving men*
> *(They taught me all I knew);*
> *Their names are What and Why and When*
> *And How and Where and Who.*

Certainly without those "serving men" no writer could function. No teacher could teach. No student could learn.

And there is something even more extraordinary. Each of those words consists of a few letters, arranged so that meaning instantly springs out of them. There are only twenty-six of these little black marks in the whole alphabet, but they are the building blocks of civilization as we know it. Infinite combinations of them contain infinite ideas. Locked inside the sentences they form are the music and the magic of written words and spoken speech.

Now and then I find myself developing a sort of foolish fondness for certain words. Take a word like *saunter,* for instance. To saunter implies a state of cheerful relaxation. No hurry, no strain, no stress. To saunter is less purposeful than to stroll, but it is not as vague as to wander or to drift. It just means ambling along, enjoying your surroundings, going no place in particular, but aware of everything.

Where does this delightful word come from? My big Webster's Dictionary says: "origin uncert." But I remember hearing somewhere that Henry Thoreau fashioned it from two French words, *sainte terre,* meaning Holy Land. Thoreau, who once said, "The swiftest traveler is he that goes afoot", must have felt that anyone who walks slowly and peacefully through the countryside looking for things to appreciate, is really making a pilgrimage in quest of the beauty and harmony that surround us all the time.

Sainte terre. Saunter. Why don't I take time out today to be a saunterer? The Spirit of Wonder may descend upon me if I do.

◇———◇

Then there are phrases so common that we seldom question them. But sometimes they contain puzzlements, too. Take the familiar exhortation to *pay attention.* Where does this idea of payment come from? Shouldn't payment, if any, come from the receiver of attention, not the giver?

Certainly the art of giving (or paying) complete attention is one of the most important skills one can acquire. I heard a story once about a patient in a mental hospital in Nebraska. He was suffering from depression so profound that he never smiled, never spoke, never responded in any way to attempts at treatment. This had been the case for years; his condition was considered hopeless.

But there was a young chaplain who, for some reason, took a special interest in this man, visited him every day, read to him, talked to him, tried to reach through to him, never gave up. It went on for months. Then one day as they both sat facing a window, just to fill the silence, the chaplain began describing the scene outside—the trees blowing in the wind, the pigeons, the squirrels. And suddenly, incredibly, a hoarse and hesitant voice spoke beside him: "I . . . had a . . . pet squirrel . . . once."

That was the breakthrough. From then on the patient began to respond. Why? Because someone paid attention. And paid it and paid it. And by so doing brought light into the darkness of a lost soul.

✦———✦

Sometimes a very small combination of little black marks may contain concepts too large for the human mind to grasp. Consider the word *time*. What is this endless flow of *something* that we all live in? Where did it begin? Where will it end? Is it just an illusion? How can one define it? Once I heard someone attempt to explain it as "one physical change measured by another." But this isn't very satisfactory. Not for me, anyway. It leaves time as mysterious as ever.

One thing seems clear about the mystery: Every day, with absolute impartiality, each of us gets exactly the same amount of time. It is almost as if some celestial being arranged to have a handsome bucket of it placed beside our bed when we wake up in the morning, with a little handwritten sign saying, "Here's your allotment for the day. What you do with it is up to you."

Sometimes I even think that this donor places *two* buckets beside our bed: one containing time; the other filled with enough energy to get through the day, solve a few problems, meet some obligations, strengthen some relationships—energy to *live* in other words. There is probably a surplus of energy, really; you can afford to dawdle a bit, dream a little, sit around with your feet up for a while, and still have enough to get by.

But the supply in the energy bucket is not limitless. If the container is riddled with little pinholes of procrastination, or really wasteful idleness, sooner or later you are going to be in trouble, because the bucket will run dry.

What's the solution? Gratitude has something to do with it, I think. Be grateful for the time you have. Be thankful for the energy you have been given. When you wake up every morning and see those two buckets standing there, make up your mind to put them to good use. Then do it!

Once in a while one encounters a handful of words, just a small handful perhaps, where the meaning is buried so deep that at first the mind is baffled. Poets have a way of doing this to us. Two lines written by Shelley once had this effect on me.

Death is the veil which those who live call life:
They sleep, and it is lifted.

The first time I read those lines they seemed to compress an idea of such magnitude into so few words that I simply couldn't grasp it. I had to read the words again and again.

But once I understood their meaning, I never forgot it. This life, Shelley is saying—the life that we are living this very moment, the life that seems so vivid and precious to us—is really blocking our vision. When we die that veil "which those who live call life" will be lifted and we will see—what? Perhaps such unimagined magnificence that our present life will seem a temporary death.

Eighteen centuries before Shelley wrote his poetry, St. Paul expressed virtually the same idea. *Now we see through a glass darkly, but then. . . .*

But then. There, truly, are seven little black marks to ponder. *But then. . . .*

Of Stars and Silence

THERE IS WONDER in words. But there can also be wonder without words, times when silence itself can be wondrous. Some philosopher—was it Emerson?—said that "silence is the element in which great things fashion themselves together." It can enhance and magnify small things too.

When I was growing up, it was traditional in some families to send young boys away to school. This happened to me and most of my friends, and I am glad it did, although I think at first I suffered from homesickness more than most. Now, of all the jumbled recollections of those years, of sports and studies and adolescent uncertainties, one fragile memory persists and does not fade, perhaps because silence was a part of it.

In our senior year, as a special privilege, some of us were allowed on certain moonlit nights in May to go down to the boathouse, take out a canoe, and carry it overland for a mile or two in the dark until we came to the upper reaches of a small but lively stream that emptied finally into the school pond not far from the boathouse where we started. Those New England nights were cool and damp. The scent of lilac was heavy on the air. Carrying the canoe was easy for us; I remember the black shadow it cast on the moonlit road, the drifting clouds overhead, and the scurry now and then of a startled rabbit in the tall grass.

As we moved along, no one said anything. When we launched the canoe and climbed in, there was no sound but the silvery drip from the paddles and the murmur of the black water as it slipped over the pebbles and tunneled its way under the overhanging branches. The whole journey took less than an hour, but there was an intimacy about it, a kind of innocence that set it apart. Behind us lay an almost completed school experience. Ahead of us lay the unknown world. Moonlight and running water and silence, with no word spoken. The *whereness* of it was unique, and therein lay the wonder.

So silence can enhance wonder, but wonder can also compel silence. Years later, Pam and I were in Yucatan, surrounded by those incredible Mayan ruins. Scientists can read their hieroglyphics, now, and tell you to the day when construction on this or that temple was started or completed, even though it was more than a thousand years ago. These people never learned to use the wheel, apparently, but they were skilled astronomers and fine architects. They are vanished now, but they left a great legacy behind.

One night there was a sound-and-light show in one of the ancient courtyards. We climbed up on some crude bleachers, lighted by feeble electric bulbs, and looked down at the tawny ruins bathed in floodlights. Someone gave a lecture on the Maya. Then when it ended, all the lights abruptly went out. We were in total darkness and a collective gasp went up, followed by a ringing silence because overhead the stars blazed down with such brilliance and intensity that they seemed almost within reach. Now we knew why the Maya were such fervent astronomers. Now we knew the wonder they must have felt. And we felt it too.

To gaze into the night sky with such intensity is a mystical experience. The Psalmist knew this well:

> *When I consider thy heavens, the work of thy fingers,*
> *the moon and the stars, which thou hast ordained,*
> *what is man that thou art mindful of him . . .*

What indeed?

There must be few among us who have never stared up at the stars and asked ourselves if some of those points of light might be suns around which revolve planets similar to our own, worlds where intelligent beings live and dream their own dreams of other inhabited spheres.

It is not simply curiosity that makes us wonder, either. When man contemplates the apparently infinite swirls of galaxies churning in endless space, he feels frightened. He wants to believe that he is not alone as his speck of dust whirls its way through the awful emptiness and the dreadful cold.

I have read the arguments of those who claim that since there is an almost infinite number of stars, then the laws of probability decree that there must be many planets similar to ours. And if this is so, the argument runs, then life as we know it must exist, or have existed, on some of them.

Indeed, if you pursue the question, you must concede that—just as we now stand on the threshold of interplanetary travel—so some older civilizations must have taken the great leap before us. You can speculate that perhaps eons ago, these beings came and looked down from their space ships at our teeming earth when the dinosaurs wallowed in the primeval swamps, and did not like what they saw, and went away.

Such fantasies are fascinating, but chances are they are only fantasies. Some scientists who have thought deeply about this feel that for intelligent life to have evolved at all required such special circumstances and so much time that the chances of such development happening elsewhere in the entire universe are very slim. Certainly not in anything remotely approaching human form.

So perhaps we are being driven back to the Biblical concept of the earth as God's particular footstool, with man His highest form of creation.

This is the impression I got from a book I read by a naturalist named Loren Eiseley who died recently. It is called *The Immense Journey,* and it talks about man's long pilgrimage in language that has great clarity and music. It talks, too, about this feeling of isolation in space and time.

In a universe whose size is beyond human imagining, where our world floats like a dust mote in the void of night, man has grown inconceivably lonely . . .

Lights come and go in the night sky. Men, troubled at last by the things they build, may toss in their sleep and dream bad dreams, or lie awake while the meteors whisper greenly overhead. But nowhere in all space or on a thousand worlds will there be men to share our loneliness. There may be wisdom; there may be power; somewhere across space great instruments, handled by strange manipulative organs, may stare vainly at our floating cloud wrack, their owners yearning as we yearn. Nevertheless, in the nature of life and in the principles of evolution we have had our answer. Of men elsewhere, and beyond, there will be none forever.

I don't presume to question or endorse Mr. Eiseley's scientific conclusions. But I'll tell you one thing. The man was a poet.

The Ultimate Reality

Advising yourself to return to wonder is one thing, doing it is another. The trouble lies not in the lack of memories, but in the abundance of them. There are so many that the choice becomes difficult.

In a way, I think the more commonplace the happening the better. Then you have to work a bit to see the miraculous and let it come through.

Perhaps what you have to do is add astonishment to ordinary cause-and-effect. For example, our old cat Casey jumps up in my lap while I am trying to read. He hooks his claws into my shirt and butts my chin with his head. His purr is a small dynamo trying to reach whatever receptors I may have to offer. Casey is not hungry; he has just been fed. He's not asking to go out; he just came in. Where is the wonder in this?

The marvel is that without being coaxed, without being bribed, this little creature with a brain not much larger than a walnut is offering me the most valuable commodity in the universe—love. If I am too jaded and indifferent to identify it, that is my loss.

But if I can put aside impatience or exasperation and say thanks by scratching Casey briefly and affectionately behind his ears, then just for a moment the barrier that separates humans from animals disappears. And that in itself is a wonder.

My old psychiatrist friend Smiley Blanton believed that these flashes of awareness are of enormous importance in determining one's outlook on life. I can still hear his voice with traces of the soft Tennessee accent that never left it: "Carlyle said that wonder is the basis of worship, and he was right. Your life will never seem empty so long as this attitude runs through it. I often say to my patients, 'If you're feeling lost or lonely or confused, let wonder open your mind to the ultimate reality, which is that all of us are part of a vast and mysterious scheme of things so comprehensive, so marvelously constructed, so generous in terms of beauty that your main response should be gratitude for being a part of it.' "

When I first met Smiley he was already famous for a book he had written called *Love or Perish*, and he believed the message in that title was literally true. While not perhaps conventionally devout, Smiley did believe in a personal God and had great respect for the insights of the Bible, to which he sometimes added his own interpretations. "What's the first verb in the Bible," he used to ask. "It's *created*, isn't it? 'In the beginning God *created* heaven and earth,' and since we're made in His image we're supposed to be creative too. When Adam and Eve were driven out of Eden, I'm sure that more than just punishment was involved. I think God knew that man needs to work and struggle and be creative, not just sit around for eternity doing nothing!"

Smiley and I worked together on a book called *Now or Never* and in the process became good friends. One reason, perhaps, was that we were both Southerners, and enjoyed legends and tall tales from that region.

"Down in Georgia," I told him once, "some folks say that if you cage a mockingbird, another mockingbird will come along and feed the prisoner a poisoned berry to put it out of its misery. Do you believe that?"

"Well, no," said Smiley. "But I must say I have a lot of patients who keep feeding themselves poisoned berries. Anger. Hatred. Jealousy. Self-doubt. Self-pity. They keep these poisons locked up inside of them and then wonder why they're sick."

"Can you usually help them?" I asked him.

"Sometimes," Smiley said. "Sometimes not. The most difficult are the ones who tell me frantically that they've tried everything possible to solve their difficulty and nothing works. So they assume nothing can work."

I was curious. "What do you say to such people?"

"Sometimes," said Smiley, "I say to them, 'Stop trying. There are great currents of love and healing flowing through this universe, but you're blocking them with all this gloom and despair.

Go home. Stay calm. Do nothing for a while. Get out of your own way. Get out of God's way. Then wait—and listen.' "

"And does it work?"

"More often than you might think," said Smiley. "Then they go around saying I cured them." He smiled his slow smile. "But you know better than that. And so do I."

I think that Smiley's exhortations to keep in touch with wonder affected me in many ways, some of them unconscious perhaps. For example, long ago I learned not to sit at my typewriter facing a window because then I spend all my time looking out. I try to arrange things so that I'm facing a nice blank wall. But gradually I begin to pin all sorts of things on the wall—photographs, newspaper clippings, cartoons, postcards, quotations, scraps of poetry, reminders to do things I never get around to doing—a chaotic collection that gets larger and larger as time goes by.

I seldom look at any item deliberately, but now and then my gaze will fall on one and stay there, as if it had something important to say to me. For example, high up on the right is a picture I cut out of some newspaper of five young children at a dance recital. All girls, from maybe five-to-eight years old, with chaplets of flowers on their heads, holding hands and skipping in a circle, smiling faces upturned, ponytails and pigtails flying. Just a newspaper photograph, but with such innocence in it and such beauty and such joy that if I look at it on the bleakest winter day, spring seems to burst into the room and stay for an instant before it is gone.

Farther down is a shimmering scene of a moonlit ocean, and underneath some words I found in Melville's *Moby Dick* where he described "one serene and moonlight night when all the waves rolled by like scrolls of silver, and, by their soft suffusing seethings, made what seemed a silvery silence, not a solitude . . ." There it all is, whenever I remember to look, in stunning alliteration that captures the magic and the mystery and the power of the sea.

Then, on the left, there is a rectangle of black paper with white lettering in some kind of antique script. I have forgotten where I found it or when I pinned it up there. The words on it are ascribed to Dame Julian of Norwich, a religious mystic who lived centuries ago, and they are arranged in eight lines. Could it be a rubbing taken from her tombstone? It seems possible, because apparently the stone-cutter forgot to put an 's' on one of the words.

BUT ALL

SHALL BE WELL

AND ALL

SHALL BE WELL

AND ALL

MANNER

OF THING

SHALL BE WELL

If I am feeling worried or discouraged and murmur those words two or three times, the shadows seem to go away.

Finally, somewhere in the clutter of mail that came not too long ago, was a reproduction of a drawing called "The Joyful Christ" by an artist named R. S. Reddick. Just a pen-and-ink sketch of the head and shoulders of a bearded young man, not looking at the viewer, but smiling at something or somebody off to the viewer's right, smiling with such warmth and spontaneity that I pinned it up on my wall so that I see it when I look up. Whenever I do, I find myself wondering what it is that he smiling about.

Is he encouraging some shy little street urchin to sit on his lap? Is he urging Martha gently not to be such a fussbudget? Has he just told the disciples that it is easier for a camel to go through the eye of a needle than for a rich man to enter the kingdom of God, and are all of them laughing because they know, as Bible scholars tell us, that the Eye of the Needle was the name for a small gate in the city wall of Jerusalem where a loaded camel did have to struggle to get through?

Or is he saying to me, "Come now, don't fret so much about the future and what it may or may not hold. Sure, you have some problems, everyone does, but you also have built into you the resources to cope with them. You pinned me up here, didn't you? So here I am, and if I can smile at your difficulties and your fears, what are you so worried about?"

Just a pen-and-ink sketch. But something in me didn't want to let it get away. Something in me wanted it up there with those other reminders of wonder. So there it remains, smiling at me right now.

How often does it have to be said? Poets and playwrights are always trying to tell us that shining fragments of the ultimate reality are all around us, all the time. Few of us who saw it will ever forget the scene in Thornton Wilder's *Our Town*, where Emily, who has died, is allowed to return to earth to watch herself as a twelve-year old girl going through an ordinary, commonplace day. Emily is so moved that she cries aloud, "Oh, earth, you're too wonderful for anybody to realize you." And that may be true. But there is no law that says we can't take my friend Smiley's advice and try, day after incredible day, to open up windows to wonder and let the magnificence of creation come streaming through.

Sharers of
Our Planet

FOR THE FIRST FEW YEARS after the war, we lived in various
places within striking distance of New York, because that was
where the editors and publishers were. The kids kept coming
along until there were five of them—four girls and finally a boy.
Sherry, the oldest girl, was separated by a few years from her siblings, Leigh, Kinzie, Dana, and Mac who were bunched together
in a kind of happy bedlam that included an endless procession
of dogs, cats, racoons, gerbils, turtles, and even more unlikely
creatures.

There was an underlying reason for all these pets. Perhaps
novelist James Michener said it best: "Every animal that walks on
earth, or swims, or flies is precious beyond description, something
so rare and wonderful that it equals the stars or the oceans or the

mind of man." Pam and I wanted some of this awareness to rub off on the children.

They were well-traveled youngsters because often during summer vacations we would pile them into the back of the station wagon and head west, looking for stories. We would usually wind up in California, which always seemed to be full of colorful characters doing unexpected things. All you had to do was talk to people. Sometimes we met celebrities. Sometimes we met people with odd professions, like the man who was the voice of Donald Duck. There were story ideas all over the place.

On one of those trips I went to see a movie producer named Ivan Tors, who was famous for his animal pictures. Our children were fascinated by Flipper the dolphin and Gentle Ben the bear, and I wondered myself what lay behind this man's extraordinary rapport with animals.

I found the genial, bearded, Hungarian-born producer at his animal ranch near Los Angeles. "Why do I make movies and TV series about animals?" he said. "The easiest answer is that I love them and have enormous respect for the simplicity and harmony and dignity they show, especially when you can observe them in their unspoiled native surroundings. But there's a deeper reason than that."

Naturally I wanted to know what this deeper reason was.

"It's my feeling," Tors said, "that to a frightening degree modern man has lost touch with nature, which means that he has lost touch with reality as God created it. He can do all sorts of complicated things with machines, but he no longer looks up at the stars, or hears the wind in the trees, or senses the rhythm of the tides. As a result, he is uneasy, unsure, full of uncertainty and anger; he has lost his sense of wonder. I think that in my films I'm trying to help him get it back."

"Some of the things your animal 'actors' do are truly remarkable," I said.

The big man laughed. "People often say, 'How do you teach those animals to do all those things?' The question they should really ask is, 'What do those animals teach you?' One thing they've taught me is how much we humans overestimate ourselves and underestimate them. Physically, we're hopelessly outclassed. A dolphin's sense of hearing is twelve times more acute than ours. One pound of lion muscle is the equivalent of five pounds of man muscle, and there are five hundred pounds in a full-grown lion. Socially, too, we humans might do well to emulate the loyalty of a dog, or the independence of a cat, or the sportsmanship of a rattlesnake that strikes only in self-defense and gives warning before it does strike."

I had to confess that I had never thought of a rattlesnake as a sportsman.

"Well, you need to learn to think like that," Ivan Tors said firmly. "Every animal can teach us something. The truth is, we're just beginning to understand animals, to know them, to make friends with them. For thousands of years, virtually all our ideas about them came from hunters; hence the term 'wild animals.' Think of the fear and prejudice the label 'killer whale' has inspired through the years. Yet when we were filming *Namu* I spent hours floating on a log beside that huge, five-ton beast, scratching his back and squeaking to him in my own version of whale talk. He was a born gentleman, the most intelligent, responsive animal I ever knew."

"It sounds as if there was real affection between the two of you," I murmured.

"Of course there was. Affection is the key word. Our whole approach to working with animals, our training methods and results, everything is based on affection. We never try to train an animal by causing fear or inflicting pain. By and large, as you know yourself, good experiences produce outgoing, relaxed, friendly people; bad experiences produce tense, suspicious, hostile ones. Animals are no different. They need love, companionship, a sense of security and enough to eat, just like the rest of us. Visitors here are astonished when they see a pretty girl, the wife of our head trainer, sitting in an enclosure with half a dozen cheetahs, scratching their ears, making them purr. But she is in no danger; the cheetahs look on her as their mother."

"Verbal communication with animals," I said, "has to be a one-way street. How do you get around that limitation?"

"We supplement it with other forms of communication, mainly touch—gentle, reassuring, loving touch. We have attendants whose main job is to pet and fondle the animals, especially the young ones. If an animal that might be dangerous is brought in, we pet him with long, sponge-tipped sticks until he becomes docile enough to touch. Even tarantulas, who are not likely to win any popularity contests, will let you tickle their tummies if you approach them calmly and gently."

Ivan Tors looked reflectively out the window at the golden California sunshine. "Dealing with animals," he said, "is a never-ending succession of wonders. And most of them are far more ready than you might suppose to deal with us. We had a dolphin named Peter, I remember, who enjoyed learning to respond to a buzzer. Peter could count very well. If we buzzed six times at him, he would buzz six times in reply. He also came very close to calling his trainer by her name, which was Margaret. He would give a prolonged squeak in which the syllables were quite recognizable.

"So even if your contact with animals is limited to a dog or a cat," said Ivan Tors in conclusion, "never take them for granted. Try to remember how extraordinary they are. Watch them. Study them. Touch them. Love them. They will expand your horizons in a most remarkable way if you do. Tell your readers that for me, will you?"

"Yes," I said, "I'll try." And I kept that promise as well as I could. Here are some of those efforts, where animals are the main actors, and people are privileged to play supporting roles.

SIDE BY SIDE

A letter came today from our friend George who lives in the shadow of the Whitestone Bridge on the edge of New York City. In one paragraph he talks about his friend Cocoa.

Cocoa is a big chocolate-colored poodle, the most remarkable dog I ever met. Whenever we would come to visit, Cocoa would astonish us by seeming to understand every word George said to her. If he wanted his shoes from upstairs, she would go and get them. If they were the wrong pair, she would take them back and bring the right ones. If George said, "Robber!" or "Crook!", she would go tearing around the house to make sure there were no intruders. Now and then I would see Cocoa and George looking at each other with affectionate amusement as if they shared a joke that none of the rest of us could understand.

But the years go by, and now George's letter says—and I know it was painful for him to write—that Cocoa has gone blind. "We've evolved a way of looping her leash (which she hasn't worn in years) loosely around her shoulders, and with this she walks confidently by my side. I can steer her either way with the slightest pressure. So there I am, a seeing-eye person for a blind dog."

Now on afternoons like today with so many angry headlines in the paper and so many small problems crowding in, I somehow find it both touching and heartening to think of my friend George and his friend Cocoa walking along tranquilly and trustfully, side by side. And I know the leash is only a symbol of the real bond between them.

The real bond is love.

Do It!

Would you think it odd if I told you that a baby raccoon once made me think of Norman Vincent Peale?

The time was several years ago. New Year's Day was approaching, and I remember asking Norman whether he could recall any resolution that had been of value to him or might be of value to others.

"Well," he said, "there's one that I do recommend to others and try to follow myself. It consists of just two words, but those words can generate enormous energy. They can sweep away discouragement and failure. The words are *do it!* Have you got a promising idea? *Do it!* Or a cherished dream? *Do it!* Or some hidden ambition? *Do it!* Don't let fear hold you back. Don't keep putting it off. Even if you think you may not succeed, *do it!* The results may surprise you."

So spoke Dr. Peale. And where does the baby raccoon fit in? I will tell you.

One morning, sitting quietly on our little dock that overlooks the tidal creek, I saw a mother raccoon lead her three babies out of the tall grass on the far side of the creek and onto a fallen tree that stretched out to deep water. She dove in gracefully and swam around, chirring at the little ones, coaxing them to join her. They just looked dismayed. Obviously, they never had tried to swim.

The mother climbed back on the tree, took one baby in her mouth, and swam across the creek with it. She did the same thing with the second. The third waited expectantly for his free ride, but nothing happened. The mother called to him from the far bank, but she didn't go back. He grew increasingly agitated, crying piteously and dipping one timid paw into the tide. The mother's answering calls became fainter. She was leaving Junior, or so she wanted him to think.

I had to admire the mother and her strategy, but I did feel sorry for Junior. Was there anything I could do to help him? Of course not. But wait a minute. *Do it, Junior,* I said to him in my mind, *just do it!* And such is the power of positive thinking, even sent by telepathy, that Junior squinched up his eyes, threw himself into the creek with a desperate plunge, and floundered frantically to the far shore where I was sure that in a moment or two he would be bragging to his siblings about how brave he was.

So you see, never underestimate the power of a New Year's resolution. Especially when it is a good one.

A Gleam of Orange

It was a stormy day along our lonely Georgia beaches. My daughter Leigh and I had planned to surf-fish, but it was too windy and too rough; no self-respecting fish would be within miles. So we walked the beach in opposite directions, looking for shells.

I was glad to be away from my desk, because I was stuck with a writing assignment that seemed to defy solution. The more I tried, the worse it got. I was discouraged, fed up, ready to abandon the whole thing. Out here on the beach, I could forget it.

When we met again at our starting point, Leigh held up a closed fist. "Look inside," she said, opening her fingers slightly. When I did, I saw something move. "What is it?" I asked, puzzled.

"A butterfly," she said. "A Monarch. She got caught in some wind blown foam and would have drowned. Her wings are too wet for her to fly. I'm going to try to dry her off."

So she did, blowing on the butterfly tenderly and very gently.

When she released the little creature, it fluttered a few yards and fell. She picked it up and tried again. Again it fell. She tried a third time, and this time with a gallant effort it soared up and away. So much heart in such a fragile body.

When we got home, the problematic writing assignment remained on my desk, and I did not go near it. But later, lying in bed that night, I remembered the Monarch soaring away on the wind. In my mind I followed that little gleam of orange until it blended with the sky. And I knew that the next day, I would try again. Yes, I would try.

Make Up Your Mind, Oreo!

This morning our big cat Oreo, so named because he is a handsome black-and-white, and I went through a familiar ritual at the back door.

Oreo has been outside for a while and he really wants to come in. So I open the door and wait. But will he come in? No. He stops and lowers his head suspiciously, as if I were some form of deadly enemy. "Come on, Oreo," I say impatiently.

He sits down thoughtfully and begins to wash his face with one paw. Maddening.

"Oreo," I say. "I give you food. I supply all your needs. If you do anything in return, I don't know what it is. Now I'm personally inviting you into my house. So come on in!"

Oreo puts one foot across the threshold, then draws it back. He looks out across the yard with some remote, unfathomable expression. He still doesn't come in.

"Oreo," I say, "I'm not going to stand here forever. If you don't come in, I'm going to close this door. This is your last chance!"

I start slowly to close the door. Does he come in? No, he sits there, exercising his free will or something. He will come in when it suits him, not before. He figures I will be patient. So far, he is right.

God made cats. He also made people. I wonder how He feels, sometimes, when He stands at the door and waits . . . and waits. . . .

The Day the Dolphins Danced

Are animals capable of feeling wonder? For a long time I never thought so, but now I'm not so sure because of something that happened a few years ago when we were on a cruise ship off the coast of Mexico.

Pam and I had chosen that ship because we knew that at about noon on a certain day its course would intersect the path of a total solar eclipse, one of those rare occasions when the moon passes across the face of the sun, covering it completely for several minutes. We hoped that good weather would enable us to see the awesome corona of the sun's rays flaming like a golden halo around the black circle of the moon. And the skies were clear.

We had expected a unique and remarkable sight. What we were not prepared for was the emotional impact. The sun and moon are so familiar that most of the time we take them for granted. But when their paths seem to cross, and eerie twilight falls, and all around the horizon the clouds glow with unearthly colors, and the planets blaze forth at noonday, and the moon's shadow races across the sea at thousands of miles an hour, the effect on the human heart is stunning.

The moon is only a barren rock, the sun a maelstrom of flaming gases. Neither has any awareness of anything. But when their meeting is ordained in the vastness of space, it is impossible to escape the conviction that a message is being sent, a statement of tremendous magnitude and majesty: "The heavens declare the glory of God; and the firmament showeth his handiwork."

And the human watchers were not the only ones spellbound. As the eclipse moved on and light began to return, a school of dolphins suddenly appeared in the ship's wake, dozens and dozens of them, leaping and cavorting joyously in and out of the silver sea. Never before had I seen so many dolphins at once, and somehow I felt an extraordinary kinship with them. "Wasn't that amazing?" they seemed to be saying. "Wasn't that a tremendous demonstration of the precision and power of this universe that we share? Won't you remember it always?"

Yes, we will.

Dr. Selye's Silver Rule for Living

L IFE IS SUCH a mysterious and complicated journey that, admit it or not, most of us are constantly looking for signposts or roadmaps to help us through it. I have had better luck than a lot of travelers because quite often interviewing people brings me into contact with such guidelines, sometimes even a whole philosophy of living.

There was the time, for instance, when I traveled to Montreal to spend a few hours with Dr. Hans Selye, the Austrian-born scientist recognized as the world's foremost authority on stress. I had long been convinced that stress was a major factor in most lives, certainly in my own. I was hoping to learn a few things that would enable me to cope with it better than I knew I did.

I liked Dr. Selye right away, there was nothing aloof or formal about him. He sat in his pleasant office in the Institute of Experimental Medicine and Surgery, relaxed and affable, his blue eyes alert and friendly behind horn-rimmed glasses. I knew that much of his work involved studying stress in animals and applying the knowledge thus gained to human problems. And so I asked him, "Have you found that stress in animals is comparable to stress in people?"

"In many ways it is," Dr. Selye said. "The stress a hungry lion feels when he can't find food is not so very different from the anxiety a factory worker has to endure when he's laid off from his job. But there are differences, too. For example, animals are free from one kind of tension that is very damaging to people. I mean the internal pressure that comes from trying to be something you're not. No animal is guilty of this, but you see it everywhere in our society. The woman of fifty who tries to look and act as if she were twenty. The businessman who poses as a great expert in his field when actually his knowledge is quite limited. Such people are under constant stress because they're always afraid of having their bluff called, or their pretense uncovered, or their inadequacy revealed." He gave me a droll look. "So try to check yourself for that now and then. You'll live a lot longer if you do."

The doctor touched a button on his desk and an attendant brought in a tray with chicken sandwiches and a bottle of white wine. I was not used to such hospitality during interviews and said so.

"Oh," said Dr. Selye with a dismissive wave of his hand, "we Viennese are charming. What's more, we know it. What's more, we use it. Charm is really a mechanism for avoiding stress, you know. It's much more comfortable to be surrounded by people who like you than by people who don't."

"That may be one way of avoiding stress," I said, "but there must be others. Do you have any advice for people who want their lives to be as free of stress as possible?"

The doctor took a sip of his wine. "Well, years ago as a young man, I felt the need to develop some kind of working philosophy of life that would keep stress at bay. And after a good deal of pondering, I think I found one."

"Would like to share it?" I asked.

"Why not?" said the doctor. "It's not difficult or complicated, really. It began with my studies in the laboratory of the basic element of life: the single cell. That cell has a quality that it shares with all living things, the quality of self-centeredness. There's no doubt that it's the instinct, and perhaps the obligation, of every organism to look out for itself. Call it self-preservation, selfishness, what you will, it's built into all of us."

"Original sin?" I suggested.

"That may be what theologians call it," said Dr. Selye. "The point is, in human society, unless this built-in selfishness is modified or controlled, it's dangerous. All great religions have known this and tried to combat it with noble principles like 'Love thy neighbor as thyself.' And much good has come from such principles. But I knew this one would never work for me because I'm not capable of loving all my neighbors."

"Neither am I," I confessed.

"Not many of us are," said the doctor. "Anyway I had to find another rule for living, one that I had some chance of obeying."

There was a knock at the door and, apologizing in English for the interruption, a white-coated laboratory technician asked the doctor several questions in German. Dr. Selye answered, then turned back to me. "Now, where were we? Oh yes, I remember. In my gropings for an effective rule for living, it seemed more and more clear to me that unless we humans surrender some of our built-in selfishness as we move through life, we arouse fear and hostility in other people—not exactly a favorable environment in which to live! Conversely, the more we modify that self-centeredness so that others love us rather than fear or hate us, the safer we are, and the less stress we have to endure."

"And your conclusion?" I prompted him.

"My conclusion," said Dr. Selye, "was that the most effective key to successful living is to persuade others to share our own natural wish for our own well-being. And this can be done only by making a constant and deliberate effort to win the affection and gratitude of your fellow man. *Earn thy neighbor's love.* Those are the four words that sum it all up. Don't try to hoard money or power. Hoard good will. Try to acquire it by doing something that helps your neighbor in his own struggle for happiness. Try to make yourself indispensable to him."

"Would it be fair to say," I asked the doctor, "that your formula is an echo of the Golden Rule? A kind of Silver Rule for living?"

"You might say that. The Golden Rule is a religious ethic. My formula emerged from the realm of biology. But there's no conflict. The results are the same. Happier people. Happier lives."

When the time came for me to go, I thanked this remarkable man for his time and his thoughts.

"Oh," he said with a smile, "they're not all my thoughts, by any means. You remember when someone complimented Montaigne on his writings, he said he had made a bouquet out of flowers from other men's gardens. All he had provided was the string. That's the way I feel about the concepts that you call my ideas. I'm just the string."

I had my doubts about that, but I kept them to myself.

"Good-bye," said Dr. Selye. "Thanks for coming. I hope some of this has been useful. And remember: Be a hoarder. That's what I am. A greedy one!"

A hoarder of good will, to make your environment less stressful. An earner of gratitude, to win friends who will support you when you need them. On the plane I thought about these things. And wondered, too, just how solid my assets were.

On the limousine ride into town, there was a woman with a heavy bag in the rack above her seat. At the terminal I lifted it down and carried it onto the platform. "Thank you," she said with a tired smile.

Her coin of gratitude made only a tiny clink as it fell into my hoard. But, I must say, it had a joyful sound.

Far Places

SOMETIMES IT SEEMS to me that there are two kinds of people: those who love a change of scene, and those who are content to remain where they are. Robert Louis Stevenson, who wrote *Treasure Island,* belonged in the first category. "For my part, I travel not to go anywhere, but to go. . . . The great affair is to move." He was also the one who wrote: "To travel hopefully is a better thing than to arrive."

Certainly if you are a seeker after wonder, you may find it in exotic places. Once in Egypt's Valley of the Kings, far underground, I remember staring up at the ceiling of some pharaoh's tomb, beautifully painted a midnight blue with the constellations etched in gold, still vivid after more than 3,000 years. Electric lights dispelling the total darkness made it possible for us to see this marvel. But where did the long-dead artists get their light? From flares of some kind? No, the guide told us, it was sunlight, pouring into the south-facing door of the tomb, then reflected by a series of polished metal mirrors around the corners of the passageways, down into the burial chamber, then up onto the ceiling. How extraordinary, I thought, how wonderful that these people, who revered the sun god, were able to bring their deity out of the sky and into this secret place.

Of course, you might argue that a housewife standing in her Connecticut flower garden, gazing at the veins of a rose petal through an ordinary magnifying glass, might be in the presence of just as much wonder, or perhaps more. No travel involved there.

But still I like to look back at recollections, some droll, some solemn, of episodes that would not have happened if I had not agreed to some extent with Stevenson that "the great thing is to move." Truth is, travel brings you into an endless variety of settings, and often it is the setting that makes the episode possible.

Here, then, are three such recollections: one from a sleepy Florida lagoon, one from a medieval German castle, and one recalling an unexpected encounter in a London hotel.

"THEY GOT ANOTHER ONE, MAMIE!"

Whenever I find myself overreacting to things, I try to recall a little episode from one of our trips to Florida. Our motel faced a quiet, saltwater lagoon. The day was hot and still. From our window, I could see an old fellow fishing from a dock not far away. Rather, he was more or less fishing. He was tilted back in a chair, hat over his eyes, apparently asleep. His tall bamboo pole was propped against the railing, line trailing in the water.

Even as I watched, a large creature of the deep—a big redfish, probably—seized the line and yanked the pole completely off the dock. Into the water it slid, where it began streaking out toward the center of the bay. I was thrilled. A small rowboat was moored to the dock. Hot pursuit would enable that lucky angler to overtake this splendid fish!

Determined not to miss a detail, I flung the window wide. As I did so, the old boy turned his head about an inch and spoke to his life companion in the house behind him. "Mamie," he said sadly, "they got another pole!"

Well, that was years ago. But to this day, when I feel my blood pressure soaring because the car battery is dead, or we are overdrawn again at the bank, or the frozen pipes have burst, or some other disaster looms, I try to remember to murmur to myself, "Mamie, they got another pole!" Then I can smile, and my blood pressure can return to normal.

Questions Without Answers

It was several years after the war in Europe ended. I was sitting in the living room of a thirteenth-century castle in Germany. It was late; everyone else had gone to bed. My host was an old Dutchman named Lodeesen whom I had known for a long time. Lodi had been a Pan-Am pilot, one of the early birds who flew the Clippers across the Pacific. On a skiing vacation in Austria he met a German war widow, a baroness whose husband had been killed on the eastern front during the war. They fell in love and married, and now were in the process of living happily ever afterward.

The family of the baroness owned this castle near Marburg. It stood all alone on a little hill overlooking a tiny village called Schweinfurt. The castle had not changed much in hundreds of years. The walls were still eleven feet thick. They even had a dungeon called the Hexenturm where they used to throw women suspected of being witches.

Here in the living room everything was quiet and peaceful. On the walls were portraits of young men in the uniforms of the German Army or Navy or Air Force. They looked happy and confident and clean-cut and alive, but I knew that most of them were dead. I also knew that I had sat in living rooms in Britain lined with almost identical portraits, except that the young men wore ribbons signifying the Military Cross or the Distinguished Flying Cross instead of the Iron Cross.

And the thought came to me that, terrible though it is in so many ways, perhaps the most terrible thing about war is that it is so seductive. To young men, anyway. Regardless of which country is right or wrong, regardless of who is said to be threatening whom, there seems to be in every nation a tremendous reservoir of something that gives human beings a willingness, an eagerness almost, to leave home, to sacrifice everything, to die if necessary when the flags fly and the bands play and a tremendous sense of urgency and purpose grips the nation. Such a force had swept up these young men smiling at me from the walls. It had swept up their counterparts in England too, and in many other nations, including my own. It had sent them out to kill one another, although they had so much in common that far more logically they should have met as friends.

Sitting there in that ringing silence, I asked myself, Must it always be so? Will memories of the pain and suffering and destruction of war fade with each new generation that comes along? Does teaching our young people to revere our war dead and celebrate the memory of old battles heighten the inevitability of another conflict? Surely patriotism and courage are virtues. How can they be retained and yet controlled, so that they do not collide fatally with those same virtues elsewhere?

With those smiling faces looking down at me and the ghosts of their owners murmuring in the shadows, I wondered—given the hideous destructiveness of modern weapons—if this might not be the crucial question facing us in the world of tomorrow. If so, where did the answers lie? In prayer? In hope? Who was to say?

Somewhere in the maze of stone corridors a clock struck midnight. I stood up and turned out the lights and went to bed.

The Bear in the Gilded Cage

Most travelers, I think, look back in terms of things they see on their journeys. But I believe the things you remember longest are often the sudden, unexpected, surprising little happenings that jolt you for half a second, out of the rut you are in, or perhaps even out of the self you normally are.

We were in London, staying in a stately old hotel with marble pillars and ornate ceilings and a slightly faded splendor. The elevator, or *lift* as they called it, was a sort of gilded cage run by a variety of liveried operators. Most were cheerful cockney types, but one was a sombre, squarish, dark-browed fellow who might have been Polish, although it was hard to tell. His English was very limited. About all he did say, every time he opened the lift door, was "Thank you, m'lady", regardless of the gender of his passenger. There was something primitive about his heavy shoulders and great clumsy paws. I thought of him, when I thought of him at all, as The Bear in the Gilded Cage.

Well, on our last day in London, I was told by higher authority that I had to buy a new coat. The one I had, she said, was old and shabby and London was the place to get a new one. I was not too pleased about this; I like old clothes much better than new. An old coat has been your friend and protector in all sorts of places. What has a new coat done for you? Nothing. What does a new fishing cap or a new hunting jacket know about the way a sea trout swims or a quail flies? Absolutely nothing. You have to teach it everything.

So I argued that there was nothing wrong with my old coat. The belt, I admitted, was a bit strange because a few years earlier in Texas I had closed the car door on it and dragged it on the ground all the way from Fort Worth to Dallas. But you could tuck that end out of sight. The rest of it, I insisted, was fine. No use. I was led forth and made to buy another one.

I brought the new coat back to the hotel in its box, still wearing the old one so that its feelings wouldn't be hurt. All the way up in the lift I was growling and grumbling that now I had two coats, and I didn't want to carry two coats home, but I didn't want to abandon my old one in cold blood and leave it in a strange land either. The result of all this was that as we left the lift, my higher authority said serenely, "Why don't you give it to him?"

I thought, what a splendid idea! If I knew where it was, and who had it, I would not mind leaving it nearly so much. So I went back into the lift and told the Bear that I had just acquired an extra coat, and that if he could use the one I was wearing he was welcome to it.

He looked at me so strangely that I decided he had not understood me at all. So I took off the coat and picked up one of his paws and draped the coat across his arm. "For you," I said. I looked up at his face, smugly pleased with my easy generosity. And saw that his eyes were full of tears.

I cannot begin to describe how that affected me. In a flash, everything was changed. I saw my own awful, casual condescension; I felt another human being's loneliness and need and isolation as if they were my own; I hated a world in which a piece of cloth could mean so little to one man and so much to another. It was cruel, it was monstrous, it was pitiful, it was unfair. And worst of all, I knew how little I was doing, day in and day out, to change it.

For maybe two seconds I stood there, frozen, looking into his eyes. Then I went on down the corridor to our room, hearing the gilded door clash softly behind us.

Oh, in the end, it turned out not to be as bleak as all that. As we were waiting for the car that would take us to the airport, in fact, the Bear came to the door of the lounge and smiled at us, and waved, and bowed, looking quite happy. And I felt happy myself, because I knew for certain that my old coat would have a good home. A very good home, after all.

A Cross in the Middle of Nowhere

IT IS SPRINGTIME in Paris. The chestnut trees are all in bloom. Along the Champs Elysées, the tulips are crimson and the grass is starred with tiny daisies. It is a good time to be alive.

I am here to do some articles for the French edition of *Reader's Digest*. My editors have asked me to go down to Burgundy and report on an unusual monastery in the little town of Taizé. The best way to get there, they say, is to take a train to Chalons, then rent a car. This means that I will have to try my trembling hand at French cross-country driving. But I am willing to risk it. My French is hardly fluent, but I figure it is good enough to get me by.

The train ride is pleasant, but when I get to Chalons there is no sign of the car I ordered. No rental car office, either. I show my confirmed reservation to the seller of train tickets, a wizened gnome with very crossed eyes.

He looks at the paper with one of them. "Ah!" He regards me sternly with the other. "You belong to Airtz."

"Airtz?"

"Oui, oui. Airtz Rent-a-Car."

"Ah! Where then is this Airtz?"

"You go all straight until you come to the Avenue de Paris. Then you go left up the hill until you see the Fiat garage."

"One can walk there?"

He shrugs. "If one wishes."

One does not wish, really, but it is a nice day and the suitcase is not too heavy, although with a typewriter added the load is not light either. I find the Avenue de Paris and trudge up the hill, past a handsome blue poster urging me to join the Communist Party for the betterment of mankind. Finally I come to a dilapidated garage. There indeed is the familiar yellow Hertz sign and inside a massive lady presiding over two tired-looking midget cars.

She shows great interest in my Georgia driving license. "This is valid anywhere in the world?"

"Absolutely!"

"But your picture looks so sad!"

"Believe me, madame, I am not like that at all."

"Ah, now I show you how to conduct the carriage."

We squeeze into the shabbier of the midget cars. She turns keys and presses buttons. Dreadful groans. Awful wheezes. Silence.

"Madame, this carriage does not march very well."

"Yes, it does. Attend one moment, m'sieu."

She clashes gears, rattles everything, the car leaps forward like a panther and stops an inch from the garage wall.

"Madame, I am the sole support of one wife, many children, two dogs, and several cats."

"In that case, I give you the other carriage, the little Primula. Much better. You will see."

This is an automotive gem from Italy. It does move forward nicely. I cannot seem to make it march backward, but no matter. I will just have to avoid dead-end streets and head-to-curb parking.

We leap into traffic in a single hair-raising bound. I try to wave goodbye with one hand to Madame Airtz. Then we are on our way, the little Primula and I.

The hills of Burgundy are full of ancient villages, remote, crumbling, drowned in time. Most of them seem the same, but one is different. It is different because, in the summer of 1940, a young student of theology from Switzerland came on his bicycle seeking solitude in which to meditate and pray. His name was Roger Schultz. What he wished to pray for was Christian unity.

Schultz was a Protestant himself, but the silent hostility between Catholics and Protestants in many Swiss communities troubled him greatly. He felt that Christ's own prayer for unity—"that they may be one, Father, as we are one"—was a command that needed to be obeyed. He was not sure how one person could have much effect. But he also knew that sometimes determined men of vision could be the hinges on which the door of history swings. His vision, fanciful though it seemed, was the eventual fusion of all the splintered churches of Christendom into one. Nothing less.

The summer of 1940 was a bitter time for France. The country was torn in two—the triumphant Nazis in the north, the dispirited Vichy government in the south. The line of demarcation ran just above Taizé. But no trains stopped there. There was no post office. The ancient Catholic church was deserted. Only a handful of inhabitants, perhaps sixty souls, remained.

For two years Roger Schultz remained in Taizé, alone but not alone because over the line came a flood of refugees, displaced homeless people, terrified Jews. Schultz took in the hungry, harried fugitives, fed them, sheltered them, tried to find places for them to go. Three times each day he prayed, alone. Local Catholics became his friends and tried to help him. In return, this unusual Protestant persuaded the priest of a nearby parish to say mass in Taizé once again. At that first service, the priest, one old woman, and Schultz were the only people in the church.

◇———◇

In 1942, while Schultz was away helping one of his refugees across the Swiss border, the Nazis poured into southern France. The first place the Gestapo went in Taizé was to his house. They closed it down. Schultz did not dare go back.

But two years later, after the liberation of France, he returned. Now three friends were with him. Their plan was to pray, to meditate, to work, to share everything, to help the poor. Food was almost non-existent; they lived on cornmeal. They washed their clothes in the village fountain. The countryside was full of abandoned children, starving, half wild. Schultz and his companions found an old house that would shelter twenty of these waifs. The first one taken in was too weak to walk, and so frightened that Schultz had to lull him to sleep by holding him in his arms and telling him stories.

By Easter of 1948, there were five in the group, and a year later the monastic Community of Taizé came into existence with seven brothers and Roger Schultz as Prior. All were convinced that their generation could no longer afford, and future generations would not forgive, a state of affairs in which Christians spent the greater part of their energy justifying positions that kept them apart from other Christians.

At the time of my visit to Taizé, there were about seventy of these calm but purposeful young men, wearing dark pullovers, dark trousers, and sandals. Brother Thomas, with horn-rimmed glasses and a Scots accent, showed me to my room, which was small but comfortable. Each brother, I was told, had a similar room which he could decorate as he pleased, with books or pictures or flowers. When the bells began to ring, I walked down to the church, joining a congregation that seemed to consist of villagers, visitors, nuns, priests, tourists with cameras, students, everybody. Some stood, some sat, everybody waited.

Worship in the church, which was built by German students as a gesture of reconciliation, is an everchanging thing. There is always serenity and simplicity, but no two services are exactly alike. The brothers come in by twos and threes in their white robes and take their places, kneeling in a semicircle. The Prior is at the far left, he is the only one who wears a crucifix. At last he rises, everyone stands, and the service begins with a burst of music from the brothers, in unison at first, then in a spine-tingling minor chord. Almost with a kind of gaiety, the congregation picks up the responses. A passage is read from the Gospel, sometimes in two or three languages. A psalm is sung. Then comes a period of silence. The coughing and rustling cease, the congregation sits in absolute stillness until the Prior ends with Christ's prayer for unity. Then the congregation drifts out onto the terrace in front of the church, where the setting sun is notched by the distant hills. The whole thing has taken less than thirty minutes.

I spent three days in this Protestant monastery, feeling its remarkable atmosphere of tranquility enfold me. I learned that more and more Taizé is becoming a place where thousands of lay men and women of all faiths come for retreats, for discussions, for encounters with other men and women hungry for Christian unity.

Sometimes they come simply out of curiosity. Often they go away changed. "The thing about Taizé," a young Italian said to me, "is that if you go there with your mind closed, something opens it. Protestants start wondering if they are right to reject everything in a tradition that, after all, their own ancestors accepted for hundreds of years. Catholics start wondering if it really makes sense to believe that there are no good Christians outside the Catholic faith. Pretty soon the things we have in common begin to seem more important than the things we don't. At home, where religion is concerned, people seem to live in the past. At Taizé they live in the future, and there's all the difference in the world."

"The main thing I learned at Taizé," said a boy from Amsterdam, "is to stop making judgments. Judging is what holds the churches apart, isn't it? Well, that's what holds people apart, too. You meet somebody, you say to yourself: 'I don't like the way he thinks, or the way he talks, or the way he lets his hair grow long.' And the moment you judge him, you're separated from him— by the barrier of judgment.

"But in this extraordinary place, nobody judges anybody. Everyone forgives everyone else in advance. So now when I go home and find myself beginning to judge people again, I try to stop. I say to myself, 'Well, that person is a child of God, just like me.' And, other people feel this, they really do. And they stop resisting you. People who've been to Taizé often think they have more power or something when they go away. But that's not really it. When you stop judging, the barriers go down, and you can move ahead faster, that's all."

◇———◇

On my last evening at Taizé, I wandered down a road, away from the crowds, trying to sort out a host of impressions, to grasp the essence of the place. It was near sundown. Along the roadside, the wild iris were spears of blue flame. An old man with a black beret and a formidable mustache wished me a good evening. He seemed inclined to talk, and after a little conversation, I asked him: "What is the meaning of Taizé?"

The question did not seem to surprise him. "Taizé," he said, "used to be nowhere. But now, you perceive, it is exactly in the center of some very important things. Above," he pointed up with a lean brown finger, "there is God. Here below," he pointed down, "is the world of men. On the one hand, but not too far, are the Catholics. On the other hand, but not too far either, are the Protestants." He paused and looked at me closely to make sure I understood. "Now, m'sieu, if you draw two straight lines, one up and down, the other running from side to side, what do you have?"

"You have a cross," I said slowly.

"Ah, m'sieu! That is Taizé!"

The Wonder of Small Wonders

Two things fill the mind with ever-increasing wonder and awe . . .
the starry heavens above me and the moral law within me.

Immanuel Kant

W HO CAN FULLY grasp the mystery of place? Why does one environment speak to us so strongly and another not at all? No one can say with certainty, but I am increasingly sure that our early surroundings condition people more than most of us realize. Climate and history, language and legend, manners and mannerisms, perhaps even the quality of light that falls on a certain place—such things leave invisible traces on the minds and hearts of those who grow up there. Indeed, for the rest of their lives, these things may act as tiny magnets drawing them back to their beginnings.

I found this to be true when I came home to Savannah for my mother's funeral. It was springtime and the old city was radiant with sunlight and flowers. The sights and smells and sounds of dozens of childhood memories came crowding back, and standing there in that peaceful cemetery I decided, almost without conscious volition, that I should come back too. It was a question of identity, of belonging. Our children were still small. Why should they not be allowed to share this sense of place that tugged at me so strongly? Or at least be able, when the time came, to choose whether they wanted to be a part of it or not?

So we did come back, and have been here ever since. We even managed, such is the pull of those invisible magnets, to acquire a small beach cottage only a few yards from the tall-roofed one I remembered so vividly as a child. So that in summers, our children were exposed to sand and saltwater, and in winters to the languid sense of heritage and history that are part of Savannah's drowsy charm.

Memories of those growing-up years remain vivid, even after all this time. Let me try to recapture a few of them. If the children's ages seem to change from one episode to another, don't be disturbed. That is what children's ages do.

BEST MEAL OF THE DAY

When we first moved back, our youngest son Mac was still a baby, with his four sisters rising ahead of him in age like a flight of stairs. Even as an infant, Mac sneered at the notion that babies are supposed to sleep for fourteen or sixteen hours; he averaged about four, mostly in the daytime. So by 7:00 A.M. on most mornings, his mother was exhausted. I was too, but being a saint at heart, I got into the habit of fixing breakfast for the other children and tossing them into the street when it was time for the school bus.

Behold me, then, on a typical school morning, attired in bathrobe with my eyes still half closed, wondering why a civilization as advanced as ours cannot invent some kind of breakfast food other than bacon, eggs, or cereal. Our oldest, Sherry, is at school in Virginia. At the kitchen table are the other three— Leigh, 9, Kinzie, 6, and Dana, 4—all meditating upon some unknown grievance or cloudy philosophy of their own. Mac is upstairs, supposedly asleep. Lucky, our apathetic black cat, is showing his only animation of the day, which means that he is hungry. I ignore him and throw some bacon into a pan.

At which point comes the first question of the morning. "Daddy," says Kinzie, "what color is Europe?"

"Syrup?" I echo stupidly.

"No, no. Europe. The State of Europe. What color is it?"

I achieve an answer that burns up half my allotted brain power for the day. "It's green in summer and brown in winter."

"Oh," says Kinzie, apparently satisfied, and I feel a little glow of triumph. But not for long.

"Daddy," says Leigh with a faraway look, "if you were an elf, how long would it take you to walk across a leaf? Twenty-four hours?"

While I wrestle with the variables in this problem, Kinzie comes to the rescue. "An elf wouldn't walk," she says loftily. "He'd fly."

"He would not!" cries Dana. "An elf doesn't have wings, does he, Daddy?"

"I don't know," I say, poking at the bacon. "I haven't seen any lately."

Silence again for a moment, except for the crunching of cereal, and then, "My toothbrush!" shrieks Dana. I wheel around, and there is Mac advancing with determined two-year-old steps. In one hand, he has a small red toothbrush; in the other, a tortured-looking tube of toothpaste.

"Oh, well," I say soothingly to Dana, "let him have it. You never use it anyway, do you?" I turn back to the bacon, which is now smoking ominously.

"I do so!" yells Dana. "Stop him!"

I turn again. Mac has a stranglehold on Lucky and is industriously brushing his teeth. Lucky's eyes are closed, his ears are flat, his fangs are (forcibly) bared in a ghastly grin. I make a lunge for Mac, but Dana beats me to it and snatches the toothbrush. Lucky streaks, foaming, through the door.

"Bloody bones!" roars Mac in a fury, his favorite oath recently acquired from Katie Morgan, a six-year-old pirate who lives down the street. He advances upon Dana with murderous intent. Dana scrambles up my back and hangs onto my ears. Leigh and Kinzie greet this accomplishment with whoops of delight. The kitchen is now filled with jet black smoke.

And so we say farewell to this lotus land of peace and enchantment.

THE DANCE OF LIFE

The third-graders were having a square dance exhibition at seven o'clock in the school auditorium, and parents were invited—no, commanded—to be there. In our house, two of the younger children wanted to go along as well, and this naturally caused some discussion.

"Gosh, Daddy," said Leigh, who was going through a phase in which she talked so fast that nobody could understand her, "we ordered 'zactly three hundred and sixty Cokes. IfKinzieandDanacome an' eachdrinksa Coke then there might be two parents whodon'tgetany Cokes and I, well, Ijust don'tknowifsmallerchildrenareinvited."

"They can bring their own Cokes," I said. "If they want to see you square dance, you ought to be pleased, don't you think?"

"Guesso," growled Leigh, parting with difficulty from her dream of having her parents all to herself for a change, watching only her, admiring only her. A human enough dream, and fragile enough to break, like most dreams, on the sharp edges of reality.

So off she went in a little while, good humor restored, bright-eyed and pretty in her wide-skirted, pink-and-white dress and white socks and black slippers. And it was just as well that Kinzie and Dana did go, because their mother didn't want to leave the baby, who had a cough. So Leigh had a family audience of three when she might have had only one.

The floor of the auditorium had been cleared, with rows of chairs around the edge for the spectators. All these were taken when we arrived, so we sat up on the stage. Kinzie was her calm, assured, six-year-old self, with occasional impish flashes in her brown eyes. Dana sat on my lap and chewed her fingers with agitation caused partly by concern for Leigh and how she would conduct herself, and partly by a burning four-year-old conviction that she could do it just as well or better if somebody would just give her the chance.

The third-graders filed in, scrubbed and solemn, and backed up against the stage. There were dozens of them: the bright lights fell on crew cuts and ponytails, blond hair, red hair, black and brown. They were not too self-conscious. Physically, they were just below the awkward age. They had not yet reached the gawkiness of young colts. They were more like a basket of half-grown kittens.

They sang some songs. "America the Beautiful," inevitably. And "Sweet and Low," too fast. Part of me was listening but part of me was already far away, running down the corridor of time, nine-years-old again, and I was singing those songs, and my parents were watching me as once they had sung the songs while their parents watched. And I had the strange feeling that time was just an illusion, and that life never really changed, only the actors were different, and not so very different at that.

The children danced their square dances, gravely and carefully.

They honored their partner, bowing and curtsying, their faces clear and young and expectant, and quite beautiful. And I felt something in my throat tighten, because I saw suddenly that the dance was a symbol of what lay before them, although none of them knew it. They would have to honor their partner later, in many ways. And they would have to match their movements to those of the people in the other corner of the square. And some would do it badly, and some would do it well. And some day, any minute now, they would sit as I was sitting, and would watch their own children dance. And perhaps they would know, briefly, this tremendous sense of life fulfilling itself, with all its hidden purpose and mystery and majesty and wonder.

Then it was over, and they went flying out like bright birds on a high note of tension-release and laughter. Leigh came swooping back to us, her face flushed with excitement and triumph.

"Gosh, Leigh," cried Dana, the openhearted, "you were wonderful!"

"Daddy," babbled Leigh, "did you see us whenwealmostgoofed? Man said promenadetotherightandwewenttothe left. Wasn't that awful?"

I said what my parents and their parents had said, and what her grandchildren would say. "It was fine, baby," I said. "Just fine."

A Whisper from Father Time

In those days the years seemed to slide by so imperceptibly that it was easy to maintain the illusion that they might go on forever.

Once in a while though, there would be a reminder that this was not necessarily so.

One summer day at the beach, when I had planned to take some of the children crabbing, I found our little boat swinging wide in deep water because the tide had come in and the wind had changed. "No problem," I said to the kids. "Wait here. I'll get it."

This was a maneuver I had not attempted for some time. On earlier occasions I would swim out, grasp the gunwale, give a quick heave with arms and shoulders, and land more or less gracefully in the boat.

So I swam out, grasped the side of the boat, and gave a confident little heave. Nothing happened. I gave a much larger heave. Still nothing. I seemed to be glued into the water, and a dark realization entered my mind. It was not Father Neptune who had me by the feet, it was Father Time. The lithe youth of yore was gone, and here was this ancient character, thirty pounds heavier, in his place.

The kids were watching with amusement. Was I going to have to beat an ignominious retreat? Then an old French proverb came to mind: *Si jeunesse savait, si viellesse pouvait,* which means, roughly, *If only youth had wisdom, if only age had strength.* "Think!" I said sternly to myself. So I thought for a while. Finally I went around to the bow, grasped the anchor rope, tied a loop in it about the size of a stirrup, put my foot in the loop, and stepped grandly into the boat.

Great applause from the shore greeted this triumph. I picked up an oar and started to paddle back, feeling quite pleased with myself. And then a faint voice sounded in my ear. "Think you're pretty smart, don't you?" said the whisper from Father Time. "Well, never mind. I can wait!"

So far, he has.

THE FISHERMAN'S TREE

One year when the hot Georgia summer ended, we stayed on in the small cottage by the sea. Nobody minded the increasingly frigid winds, certainly not my British-born wife with her love of blustery weather. But as Christmas drew near, the children began to worry about a tree. Usually we went out into the woods and cut our own Christmas tree, but there were no pines along the lonely beaches, just scrub palmetto and a few stunted oaks. And it was unlikely that commercial evergreens would find their way into our little seaside community.

"It's just a fishing village," I told the children at supper one night. "Nobody will be selling Christmas trees."

"Maybe we should have a fisherman's tree," our youngest said pensively. "Jesus liked to fish, you know."

"Did not!" said one of his sisters scornfully.

"Did so! He told the disciples where to put their nets and they caught a lot of fish. A hundred and fifty-three. It's in the Bible. They showed us in Sunday school."

"Well, how would you make one, smarty?"

"I don't know," our Bible scholar confessed. "We'd all have to think."

So we all thought, and gradually—out of nowhere, really—the fisherman's tree took shape.

First we took a cast net, my big mullet net with a diameter of 14 feet. We hung it from the porch ceiling and arranged the heavy sinkers around a circular coffee table about five feet wide. That gave us a proper Christmas tree shape, and a very graceful one at that.

At the top of the net, we fastened a large starfish that we had brought home from the Bahamas, and on the table, visible through the mesh, we placed a small creche, complete with the holy family in a stable and shepherds kneeling around. We didn't have any wise men, but we mounded beach sand over the table top to make it look like a desert, with small branches of sea oats for palm trees, and mysterious marks that our youngest said were camel tracks.

The sea itself supplied the decorations. The girls brought home sand dollars and sprayed them with gold or silver paint. We all combed the beach for bits of coral and ropes of seaweed, fragments of sponges and miniature horseshoe crabs, mother-of-pearl interiors from clamshells and golden-throated conchs. We knew a secret place where a dredge had sucked up sand from deep below the ocean floor. In the sand were fossilized sharks' teeth left there eons ago, smooth as glass, some still sharp as razors. They reflected the light like tiny polished mirrors, and because they were rare and sought after, we placed them by the creche to symbolize the gold and frankincense and myrrh.

Sand dollars, you know, have a little five-pointed star inside, breakable into fragments that look exactly like white doves with outspread wings, so we put some of these on the roof of the stable. We had no angels, but we had plenty of angel wings, those delicate ovals of fluted calcium that all shell collectors know. We taped them to the net, and high among them, our tallest girl placed one little dried sea horse, sprayed silver, who hung by his tail and swayed contentedly in the ocean wind. We had no Christmas lights, but we had one magnificent glass globe, flotsam from a Japanese fishing trawler, that came bounding ashore one day when I was surf fishing alone, its rope netting encrusted with tiny lavender mussel shells. When we put a spotlight behind it, the light that came through was a pure, almost mystical, aquamarine.

Everyone liked the tree except our crusty old neighbor Mrs. Henley. "Outlandish!" she said. "What kind of Christmas tree is that? Why, it isn't even green!" But we knew that Mrs. Henley loved to spread gloom, even at Christmastime. So nobody paid her any mind.

Why am I telling you all this? There is no story here, I know. Nothing dramatic happens; it is just a recollection. But somehow even after all these years, there is an element of wonder in it.

One frosty night, I remember, when the children were all asleep, I went out on the porch to turn off the spotlight. The moon, three days past full, was just rising out of the sea, streaking the dunes with black and silver shadows. I turned off the light, but the little creche still glimmered against the sand, and over it hovered our Christmas tree that had suffered "a sea change, into something rich and strange." I stood with the porch floor cold under my bare feet and watched it for a long time.

So Christmas comes again with all its warmth and color and magic. We're back in the city now, and I am sure that this year we will have a traditional evergreen, its branches weighted with bright baubles taken from boxes. A lovely thing to pile presents under, and yet. . . .

Somehow the memory keeps coming back, so very real under the overlay of time. The children are all young again, and asleep in their beds. The restless sea is touched by the moon's pale fire. And the fisherman's tree stands quietly with the starfish at the top, and the sea horse swinging like a cheerful question mark, and the clean smell of salt and seaweed, and the sharks' teeth like dark arrowheads against the sand. As the poet wrote, these are memories that—

> *I keep forever, like the sea-lion's tusk*
> *The broken sailor brings away to land*
> *But when he touches it he smells the musk*
> *And the whole sea lies hollow in his hand . . .*

Just as the whole world once lay in the hollow of a Baby's hand. So many Christmases ago.

Bread Upon the Waters

DOES SOME SORT OF special wisdom descend on those of us who manage to reach our eighth or ninth decade more or less intact? I doubt it, although at times some of us act as if it does. The most I care to claim is that as the years pass some early perceptions that were vague or hesitant begin to be seen more clearly.

One such perception is that the major patterns of life have a tendency to repeat themselves. For example, Pam and I lived through a war, had a handful of children, and thought that was that. But then we found ourselves with another set of children, not bound to us biologically, but certainly emotionally, living through yet another war. Is there a reason for such things? Probably, although sometimes it can be discerned only dimly.

In this case, perhaps there is a clue in that cryptic admonition in the Bible: *Cast thy bread upon the waters, for thou shalt find it after many days.* I think the Preacher (that's how the writer of Ecclesiastes refers to himself) seems to be saying, "Do something generous now and then. Do it even if it seems a bit foolish or reckless, because when you do, you set in motion the great Law of the Echo that runs like an invisible current through the scheme of things. That current may seem to flow away from you in the beginning, but it can reverse itself, and often does, after many days."

The 1970s brought a new and unforeseen element into our lives in the form of visitors from a very different culture. They were Vietnamese helicopter pilots who came to be trained not far from where we live. Our military people asked us to welcome these young men by taking them into our home when they had any free time and helping them with whatever problems they might have. We took them in pairs, each pair leaving us on graduation and returning to duty in Vietnam. We had four pairs over a period of two years and became very fond of them. They called us Maman and Papa, and we thought of them as our children.

Casualties among these pilots were high, and we worried about them a great deal. By the time the war ended, we figured about half of the American-trained pilots were either dead or missing. If a few managed to escape, we told ourselves hopefully, we might hear from one or two.

The first one we heard from was Hap, bright-eyed inquisitive Hap. Late in April, when Saigon fell and the Viet Cong broke through the perimeter of their base, he and three other pilots made a dash for Hap's helicopter, took off in a hail of gunfire, flew out to sea, landed on an American aircraft carrier, and eventually were brought to Eglin Air Force Base in Florida.

I was in New York when Pam called from Savannah. "Hap's made it!" she said. "He's at Eglin. He wants to come back to us. If we'll agree to sponsor him, they'll let him come as soon as he can get security clearance."

Sponsorship, I knew, meant a commitment to feed, clothe, and shelter a refugee until he became self-supporting. "Send him his bus fare," I said. "What does he say about Cuong and Hung and the rest?"

"He thinks Cuong may have gotten out. He's afraid Hung may be dead. Hap's own brother was shot and killed when he tried to escape by boat. Oh, they've all had such a terrible time!"

A few days later, another telephone call came. From Guam, this time. "Maman," said the faraway voice, "it's Cuong . . ."

Cuong. One of the first two pilots we had known. Taller than most Vietnamese, reserved, with a sensitive, serious face.

Now it was difficult to understand him, his English was rusty, and the connection was bad. Apparently he had been able to fly his helicopter into Saigon, land near his home, pick up his wife, their 10-month-old baby, and some other members of his family. They had landed on an American ship and been transferred to a freighter crammed with 8,000 evacuees. For three days and three nights his wife had held their baby in her arms, with no room to lie down and just half a cup of rice each morning and half a cup at night. They had been told that they might be sent to New Zealand, but they did not want to go there. Could they somehow come home to us?

"It's all right," Pam kept saying. "We love you. We'll see you soon. We'll send a telegram saying we're willing to sponsor you and your family."

We sent the telegram, and letters too, but in the chaotic conditions on Guam they were never delivered, and as the days went by Cuong began to despair:

Dear Maman and Papa,

I've been here 14 days in waiting for your letter message but up-to-day not at all.

Maman and Papa, the terrible dream had passed but the near future in front of us is a worry anxiety. So I will need your help, your recommendation. Please tell my wife you love her and make her calm in soul. After five years, I still live in a terrible war, survive in many many cases, I only know a way and look forward the God and thank.

Maman and Papa, I want to cry myself.

Your unfortunate son,
Cuong.

Hang in there, Cuong, I said to him in my mind when I got his letter. And it was not the first time.

Even when he was still in training, I knew that Cuong detested war. He wanted to be an electrical engineer, not the commander of an insane machine that spewed out death, or else spent its time carrying whole men into battle and bringing them out maimed and bleeding and dying. He hated to kill anything. I took him dove hunting once. "Oh," he would cry gleefully after each futile shot, "I am so shameful!" But I knew he was missing on purpose.

English never came easy to Cuong, but sometimes, despite the language barrier, the poet in him would struggle through. At his graduation ceremony, where we exchanged programs, he wrote these lines on his:

I don't really know how to express my feeling but of what you think about a flower blossom in a early pure morning that my sympathy proudly comes out in my heart since I luckily met both of you. And now, I am just able to say that the words I usually call to my Parents I am proud to call you both with that lovely term.

Your son,
Cuong.

Back in Vietnam, flying endless hours of combat, Cuong was often disheartened. He had a girl named Tuyet, but felt he should not marry her "for the reason of, close of death, I don't want to make anybody painful of me." Eventually he did marry her, but his letters remained somber.

About all we could do was send back words of encouragement. Some of our letters he received, some he did not. "Don't let your troubles overwhelm you," I wrote. "Someday this madman's war will end. Someday you will have children of your own. Someday you will see us again." I don't know how I was so certain of these things. But I was.

And I was right, because the day finally came when Cuong and his family arrived at a refugee camp in Pennsylvania, and made contact with us through the International Rescue Committee. "We'll send them on to Savannah as soon as possible," the I.R.C. worker said on the telephone. She hesitated. "Cuong has a close friend here, a pilot named Thach. He has no sponsor . . ." Her voice trailed off.

"Well," I said, "send him along."

I was still in New York when Cuong arrived in Savannah. With him were his gentle wife with the lovely name of Bach Tuyet (meaning "White Snow"), their 11 1/2-month-old son Truc, Cuong's 20-year-old sister Nhung (pronounced Nyung), his brother Nghia (Neeya), who was also a helicopter pilot, and Thach (Tac). When I called home that night, the background noises sounded as though they were straight out of Saigon. "How are things?" I asked Pam.

"Wonderful," she said. "They're just great. I love them all."

"How's the baby?"

"Adorable. He looks like a Mandarin doll. We're teaching him to say 'Bye-bye.' "

"What's he doing now?"

"He's playing on the floor with Hap and Charlie." (Charlie was our one-eyed, more or less Siamese cat.) "He pulls Charlie's tail, but Charlie doesn't mind because they're both Orientals."

"How are the others?"

"Fine. They're all planning a great celebration dinner for you when you come home."

Memorable indeed was that dinner, the food an exquisite blend of French and Chinese cuisine, the menu carefully hand written and propped against my glass with each course numbered: 1. *Shrimps-swim-in-the-ocean* (a delicious sea-food soup); 2. *Green-garden* (a salad); and so on to the end, where it simply said, *Thank you too much.*

Above the mantel, the portrait of a man with a general's stars on his shoulders looked down from the shadows and someone asked about him. "That's my grandfather," I said. "He also had four years of war. And the South lost that one, too. When he came home, he had a ragged uniform and a small Italian coin dated 1863. Nothing else, except a wife and two babies waiting for him. But he lived through it. They built their lives again."

"Maybe someone help them," Nghia murmured. "Now you pay back debt."

No such thought had crossed my mind. "Maybe so," I said. *Cast thy bread. . . .*

I looked at the grave young faces around the table, faces from half a world away, and wondered how they had managed to survive as well as they had. I thought of that late afternoon in Saigon, with the enemy closing in, when Cuong's helicopter came clattering over the house where his family waited for this prearranged signal. They all raced to the tiny landing area they had agreed upon, carrying nothing except the clothes they wore and milk for the baby. The area was so small that the chopper had to take off vertically, which meant that the load was limited and not everyone could go. Cuong's youngest brother Thi volunteered to remain behind with his wife and baby, as did Cuong's father, whom he loved so much.

Now the survivors were here around our peaceful table. There sat Cuong, quieter, more mature, the head of his family now. There was Nghia, whose wife and baby were still somewhere in South Vietnam. There was Nhung, shy and graceful as a fawn, and Tuyet minding the baby while the rest of us ate.

And there was our new friend Thach, with his strong, sad face full of patience and endurance. It was Thach who flew 26 people he did not even know to freedom, in a helicopter designed to carry ten or twelve at the most. When he reached an American ship, two American choppers were preparing to fly to the American Embassy in Saigon to bring out the remaining American personnel. But the Viet Cong had control of most of the doomed city, and the groundfire might be intense. They asked Thach if he knew of an approach that might be less dangerous than others, and, if so, whether he would fly his own helicopter back and guide the Americans. In other words, having just escaped from hell, would he mind stepping back in?

Thach led the American choppers in safely. On his second flight out, he brought a single Vietnamese with him, the only one he could find. I wondered if anyone bothered to thank him before they pushed his helicopter into the sea to make room for others that were straggling in.

Outside, the brief Georgia twilight was fading. November was far away, but I knew that we had just had our Thanksgiving dinner for this year. "Shrimps-swim-in-the-ocean" instead of turkey; "green-garden" instead of cranberry sauce. But the real Thanksgiving ingredients—closeness and caring and a deep sense of relief and gratitude—were all around us, warm and strong.

After dinner, the kitchen seemed crowded with people. Truc and Charlie were on the floor contemplating each other with mutual admiration. Hap was telling Pam's fortune with a pack of cards. Nghia was teasing his sister about something in melodic Vietnamese. Nhung's lovely ivory face was alight with laughter. Thach was carrying dishes from the dining room, Cuong and Tuyet were putting them in the dishwasher.

The moment caught and held and I knew I would remember it always. At least they are alive, I thought, at least they are here.

Little Truc left the cat and crawled over to the foot of my chair. He sat up and looked at me with eyes as dark as forest pools. Slowly, he raised one tiny hand and waved it hesitantly. "Bye-bye?" he said.

I reached out and touched his velvety little fingers. "Not really, Truc," I said. "From now on, it's all hello."

That is how it has been ever since. Truc is now in college in California. Cuong and Tuyet have just bought a larger furniture store, and Tuyet has gone back to visit relatives in Vietnam. Nhung and Thach are married and have two remarkably bright children.

Hung was not dead after all. The Communists caught him and threw him into a concentration camp where he was held for six years and almost died. His wife Mai was allowed to visit him twice each year, for fifteen minutes each time. He was allowed to kiss her goodbye, and at one point was able to push a note into her mouth with his tongue. The note, addressed to me, said he did not expect to live, but hoped that somehow we would be able to help his wife and small daughter. We tried for years, with no luck. But now Hung and Mai are living only a few blocks away from us, and their little girl has entered college. *Thou shalt find it after many days. . . .*

A year or two ago, one of our own children—it was Mac—went to California for some postgraduate study. He got a student loan for his tuition, but he and his equally impoverished roommates had little else. They rented a house with no furniture and slept on mattresses. They ate sitting on the floor in the kitchen.

Then one day a truck pulled up, crammed with brand-new furniture: a bed for our son, a diningroom table and chairs, a sofa and armchairs, lamps, everything. No payment required, none would be accepted. The young students were amazed and delighted. When Pam called to express our appreciation, Tuyet just laughed her silvery laugh. "No, no Manan! In my country, parents never thank children. Don't worry. We take care of our little brother!"

Her "little brother" is six-feet-two, and his skin color is different, but the Preacher was right: Cast the bread of kindness upon the waters of life, and it will return to you—one way or another—after many days.

When a Portrait Comes to Life

THERE ARE TIMES when I wonder what it was like a few generations ago when families were much larger, when sometimes grandparents or even great-grandparents—not to mention great-uncles and great-aunts—lived under the same roof with teen-agers and toddlers and harassed parents. Was there really more warmth and caring and sharing than there is today? Was there a stronger sense of life as a continuum, with each individual a link in an endless chain reaching back into the past and stretching out to the future? Who can say?

The way we live now, ancestors tend to fade very quickly, we hardly know them at all. But now and then one will step out of the shadows to remind us that they did precede us, that they were real people of flesh and blood, and that in a deep invisible sense they are still living in us today.

In the last chapter I mentioned a portrait in our dining room, looking down at our Vietnamese children and ourselves. Just a two-dimensional likeness of a man I never saw in actuality. But last night, for a little while. . . .

◇——————◇

Sometimes, late at night when the house is still, I like to pull a book at random from the shelf. Any book, so long as it is old. I open it at any page and read a few paragraphs. If what I read bores me, I put it back. If not, I keep reading for a while.

I don't know exactly why I do this. Maybe it is an antidote to television. Or maybe I think I gain some perspective from it. We are so accustomed to living in the immediate present that our personal problems often seem enormous, overwhelming, all-important. But when the past comes alive for you, even momentarily, you realize that there is nothing new about your troubles. And nothing permanent, either. A hundred years from now, they will be as dry and dusty and forgotten as the printed page you are holding in your hand.

Last night the book I chose was an old biography of J.E.B. Stuart, the great Confederate cavalry leader, published in 1885. It fell open at page 44, which described an artillery duel near Dranesville a few days before Christmas, 1861. In the margin was a laconic note in pencil: "We were close by; this was the first time I saw a shot cut a man's head entirely off his body."

And a few pages farther on another note: "Our Negro grooms witnessed this fighting, and enjoyed it until some bullets whistled near us, whereupon my groom said, 'Let's us go somewheres else, Lieutenant; dem Yankees jes' as soon shoot me as you!'"

So it went, page after page, the brief marginal comments of someone who had seen the Civil War, not as a historian or an onlooker, but as a participant.

There were no elaborate descriptions, just penciled notes. Of the famous ride around McClellan, for example: "It was 60 hours from 3 A.M. Thursday to daylight Sunday, and the Hussars were in the saddle all that time except about one hour at Tunstall's and two hours while we were building a bridge."

Sixty hours in the saddle. I tried to visualize how he must have looked, how they all must have looked: the pale, stubbled faces gray with fatigue, but full of elation, too. Why not? They had ridden around the whole damn' Union Army, hadn't they, with the loss of only one man? When a swollen river trapped them, with the Yankees coming on behind, they had fought off their pursuers and built a bridge and got clean away.

"If you want to have a good time, jine the cavalry. . . ." That was Stuart's favorite song, until he was brought down at Yellow Tavern three years later with a Yankee pistol ball through his body. Where he said to his confused and disheartened men, "Go back! Go back and do your duty as I have done mine, and our country will be safe. Go back! I had rather die than be whipped!" And they did fight on, for a while.

I knew that the man who had written the notes in this book was very small, because a few years ago I came across his Confederate overcoat and tried to put it on, and could not even get my arms into it. I knew that he came back from the war penniless, to a town occupied by the enemy. I knew that in the years that followed he rebuilt his business, raised six children, and did what he could for his town. When the terrible epidemic of yellow fever came in '76, he sent his family away, but stayed behind himself to nurse the sick and the dying. He was so sure that he would die himself that he wrote a sealed letter, saying goodbye to his wife. But he lived through it.

He must have been a good soldier, because in 1898 he became a general in the Army he had fought against through the four long years of civil war. After the war with Spain ended, he returned once more to civilian life. Ten years later, a sitting President of the United States came to stay at his house. They drove together through streets decorated with gay bunting. It was raining, and some of the colors in the flags had run. President Taft remarked that this was a pity.

"Yes," said his host with a smile. "We should have used Confederate colors. They never did run."

I never saw this little man, he died the summer I was born. And I must confess that to me, through most of these years, he has just been a portrait on the wall. But last night, in the quiet around midnight, for a little while he became very real. You might almost say that last night, in the pages of an old book, I met my grandfather for the first time.

Why do these memories of a far-off war still have so much power to touch the heart? I think I know why. It is because those people in those times were deeply acquainted with a word that in our time has become dusty with disuse. The word is *honor*. They knew what it was, they believed in it, they fought to keep it in their lives, and when those lives ended, they wanted to die with it.

Listen again to the words of the dying Stuart. He knew the war was lost, but honor was not lost. "Go back and do your duty as I have done mine." That was the creed on both sides, and it shines through all bickering and acrimony that have arisen today.

I have never forgotten the Union General Joshua Chamberlain's written description of the final surrender of the battered Confederate forces at Appomattox in 1865. Wounded six times in the war and holder of the Congressional Medal of Honor, Chamberlain was designated to receive the actual surrender. His troops were lined up in battle array. The defeated Confederates would march past and lay down their arms. It was the end of four years of bitter struggle and untold bloodshed. Although he knew he would be criticized (and later was), Chamberlain had given orders to his troops not only to refrain from cheers, but when the defeated enemy came past, to salute "these men, now thin, worn, and famished, but erect with eyes looking into ours, waking memories that bound us together as no other bond."

At the head of the gray column was General John B. Gordon, one of the last of Lee's lieutenants who himself had been wounded five times in one day during the furious battle at Antietam. Now let Chamberlain describe the scene:

Our bugle sounds the signal and instantly our whole line from right to left gives the soldier's salutation, the marching salute. Gordon at the head of the column, riding with heavy spirit and downcast face, catches the sound of shifting arms, looks up and, taking the meaning, wheels superbly, making with himself and his horse one uplifted figure, with profound salutation as he drops the point of his sword to the boot-toe; then, facing his own command, gives word for his successive brigades to pass us with the same position of the manual—honor answering honor. On our part not a sound of trumpet more, nor roll of drum; not a cheer, nor word, nor whisper of vain-glorying, but an awed stillness rather, as if it were the passing of the dead.

With what strange emotion I look into these faces. It is by miracles that we have lived to see this day, any of us standing here. How could we help falling on our knees, all of us together, and praying God to pity and forgive us all!

Honor, pride, courage, and forgiveness—what a legacy for all of us today, if only we were wise enough to accept it.

The Amen Corner

Just off one corner of the old dock I told you about is a deep hole much favored by blue crabs, or even sometimes a stone crab or two. If you toss a baited crab-basket there, wait a while and then retrieve it, chances are you will have the beginnings of a crab stew, or at least a crab cocktail. The children always said that if you prayed for good luck while you were waiting, it helped. So that section of the dock's railing became known as the Amen Corner, this being the proper way to end prayers if you want them to be heard.

I like to go down to the Amen Corner early in the morning sometimes, and just lean against the weathered railing, and watch the green ocean water come swirling slowly along the marshes and the mudflats on the flood tide. On these occasions, I have found that if I make my mind as blank as possible—not too difficult as a rule—sooner or later some interesting idea or association is likely to leap into it.

The other morning while I was watching some mullet jump in a swirl of bubbles on the far side of the creek, four lines of verse eased into my head:

> *Life is mostly froth and bubbles.*
> *Two things stand like stone:*
> *Kindness in another's troubles;*
> *Courage in your own.*

The story in the family was that Aunt Daisy saw these words inscribed below the mantelpiece of a manor house in England, and brought them home with the thought of making them available to her Girl Scouts. My father looked up the author, a Victorian poet named Adam Lindsay Gordon. "If you need a rule to live by," Father used to say, "you won't find a better one than that. Not in eight words, anyway."

Thinking about Aunt Daisy and Father drew another scene to the surface from out of the well of the past. The place was the dining room of our old house on Oglethorpe Avenue. The time was Easter morning. I was eight or nine, and I had a new blue tie for Easter, but I was feeling uneasy because I also had a mite box problem.

Mite boxes, in case you have forgotten or never knew, were small cardboard containers we children were given at the beginning of Lent. During those forty days, each of us was supposed to put coins through the slot in our mite box—money from our allowance or any other source—to be handed in on Easter morning at church as an offering of self-denial.

My thirteen-year old sister was very good about putting coins in her mite box. I was pretty good too. The trouble in my case was that sometimes in moments of acute financial need, I would pry some of the coins out of the box. My conscience gnawed at me a bit, but not too severely, because I always intended to put the money back before Easter morning. And somehow never did.

Well, the morning came, and with it came Aunt Daisy who planned to go to church with us after breakfast. When we brought our mite boxes to the table for inspection, my sister's was clean and plump and heavy with nickels and dimes. Mine was smudged and dog-eared from illicit openings; inside a few surviving pennies rattled forlornly.

My father, who knew how wicked I was, gave me quite a lecture. Why was I so selfish? Why couldn't I think less about myself and more about others? He was intent on making me feel guilty, and he did.

Finally Aunt Daisy fished in her purse and drew out a fifty-cent piece that looked to my dazzled eyes as large as a washtub. "Here," she said to me. "Put this in your mite box."

"Not fair!" howled my sister.

"It's not right, Daisy," Father said stiffly. "The boy shouldn't be rewarded for poor performance."

Aunt Daisy smiled at both of them. To my sister she said, "You're right, dear, it's not fair. But never mind, God knows how faithful you've been." To my father she said, "Haven't you ever had a gift that was undeserved? I should think Easter would remind you of that."

Then her warm brown eyes rested on me. "God loves all sinners," my favorite aunt said serenely. "Large ones and small ones. But don't push Him too far."

Standing there on the old dock, after all these years, I remembered her advice. Then, across the creek a mullet jumped again, and I left the Amen Corner and went back up the path to the house.

Reaching Back for Wonder

ITHINK IT'S a great pity that people so seldom write letters nowadays. Real letters, I mean, personal letters. Electronics have taken over, I know. Easier? Yes. Faster? Certainly. But somehow dehumanized, too.

Before I was born, when my Savannah grandmother had married children living in England, she was quite capable of sending someone to the post office two or three times a day to check on incoming transatlantic mail. Those letters were at least a week old, sometimes two, but they were longed for with unwavering intensity. And there was always a deep feeling of pleasure and fulfillment when they did come. It was communication, satisfying and intimate and wonderful and human.

Today and every day, our cheerful postman, whose name is Carl, comes down our street loaded with mail, most of which is hardly worth delivering—catalogues and bills and appeals for charities and sweepstakes flyers and so on. So my anticipation is never very high. I always know when Carl is approaching because the silly dog named Alfred who lives next door barks hysterically, as if he had never seen Carl before. Most of the time, I just try to tune Alfred out, and Carl does too. "He has to earn his dog bisquits somehow," says Carl tolerantly.

This past week I have been listening for Carl more attentively than usual because I have been waiting to hear from the kids. Old Smiley Blanton, whom I have quoted so often, had no children of his own, but he had firm advice for those who did. "Don't worry about giving your children toys and games and such," he used to say. "Make it your job to put them in contact with the marvelous. Your own life will be richer if you do."

Pam and I tried to do this with our five, never quite knowing whether we were succeeding or not. Then the other day, just for fun and with this book on my mind, I decided to ask each of them to try to recall a moment of wonder from childhood, write it down, and send it to me. It took a few days, but finally I heard from all five of them. I thought their answers might include such impressive things as their first sight of the Grand Canyon, or the sound of a symphony orchestra. But I was wrong, the moments they recalled were smaller and more intimate.

Writing from Atlanta, Sherry remembered pouring a packet of seeds into the crude "garden" she had scooped out of some very unpromising dirt behind the garage. "I never expected any flowers to come up," she wrote. "When they did, I was overwhelmed by the mystery of creation. To this day, forty years later, the smell of zinnias and marigolds transports me back to my secret garden."

Leigh recalled finding a bird's nest when she was three or four with baby birds in it. "They were so fragile, but so alive, with those mouths wide open, as if they expected me to bring them a worm!"

Out in Colorado, Kinzie remembered the contrast between the immensity of the sea and delicacy of some of the creatures it contained: "Tiny seahorses and horseshoe crabs the size of a dime. The thrill and challenge of beachcombing for these perfect little things carried me into archaeology, and years later my findings in that discipline gave me the same feeling." She added a wry postscript. "Of course, the real wonder came on those rare occasions when one of my siblings said something nice about me!"

Dana wrote about "nights on the flat roof of our old beach cottage waiting to catch a glimpse of Sputnik. It was just a tiny spark moving across the heavens, but to me it was more mysterious and marvelous than all the later space triumphs combined. It was our very own human-made star up there with all the billions of stars that had been shining for billions of years. If wonder is a sensation that makes your scalp tighten and leaves a hollow emptiness in the pit of your stomach, that is what I felt."

Far away in California, Mac wrote that he looked back with wonder on the patience of parents, including, fortunately, his own. "Fishing in the surf when we were too small to cast a line, you'd cast it for us. Despite your instructions, we'd reel it in instantly whether we had a bite or not, and you'd have to zing it out all over again. Somebody asked you if this wasn't a waste of time, but you said no, it wasn't, because each time we learned more about currents and wave action and how to tell the difference between vibrations from the bottom and a real fish's bite. I try to remember that sometimes when I find my own patience wearing thin."

I smiled over those letters, but I also felt a sense of relief and happiness, because I knew what they were really saying. They were saying that all children are instinctive seekers of wonder, that all parents have to do is encourage them to be a bit adventurous.

And then stay out of the way.

Swing Low

THE WORD "aging" has a gloomy sound, don't you agree? Oh, it is fine when applied to cheese or wine. But to human beings? There it has all sorts of melancholy connotations, seems to me.

Perhaps I am wrong about this. In the days when I worked closely with Smiley Blanton, he was nearing eighty, but it did not seem to bother him. Every age, he said, has its advantages, pleasures, limitations, and compensations, the important thing is to recognize this and act accordingly. Moving into your seventies, eighties, or even nineties can be very pleasant, Smiley said. "You no longer find it necessary to impress people with how important you are. You can say exactly what you think about modern art. If opera bores you, you can proclaim the same without guilt or explanation. It's all really quite nice."

Well, perhaps it is nice if you manage to retain a reasonable amount of health and vitality as you traverse these golden years. But how do you do that? Is it all pre-programmed into your genetic code? Or does your state of mind have something to do with it?

Once I asked a preacher-friend, well into his eighties but still full of humor and enthusiasm, how he kept those qualities alive so successfully. He smiled and said, "We're all creatures, remember. And the Power that created us is still with us, still available as it has been all along. Stay close to that Power, have faith in it, draw strength from it. That's the secret. Nothing more."

One morning not long ago, I went out to Laurel Grove to visit the graves of my parents and grandparents. It is a very old burial ground with streamers of Spanish moss weeping over tilted tombstones and dust motes hanging in the shafts of sunlight. The sense of timelessness is very strong.

Far back in the days when I was growing up at our beach cottage, we had a wonderful black cook named Charlotte. Charlotte never let anything bother her; she just stayed serenely in her kitchen singing old songs in a rich contralto voice that came floating up the dumbwaiter shaft along with marvelous smells of cornbread and such. One of her favorites was "Standin' in the Need of Prayer." another was "Swing Low, Sweet Chariot," and it was from this one that I got the idea that my forebears were not really in Laurel Grove, because they had been transported angelically elsewhere long ago.

I looked over Jordan, and what did I see,
Comin' for to carry me home?
A band of angels, a-comin' after me,
Comin' for to carry me home.
Swing low, sweet chariot. . . .

So I knew my parents and grandparents were not there, but
something in me wanted to make sure nothing had changed.

Now, passing under the old wrought-iron arch above the entrance to Laurel Grove, I began looking for the tops of the towering magnolia trees in our family plot, because unless you have
a landmark, it is hard to find anything in the maze of winding
lanes that make up most of the cemetery. Those trees were
planted long ago, one at each corner of the lot, by some forgotten ancestor. Now they are at least sixty feet high. Their gnarled
roots have so emphatically displaced the foundations of the iron
fence that everything is crooked and the gate will not work. To
repair the gate and the fence, you would have to take down the
trees. But this would be a sacrilege, and certainly frowned upon
by the old owl who lives in one of them. A few years ago I tried
to compromise by having the fence painted, even if it was askew.
But then it looked so shiny and peculiar, compared to everything
else, that I almost wished I hadn't done it.

It is always very quiet in Laurel Grove, nobody is ever around.
I forced open the reluctant gate and went over and sat on the edge
of my grandfather's tombstone with its cavalry sabre in *bas relief*
on the marble. I didn't think he would mind, since he wasn't

there. Everything looked familiar and unchanged. Mother and Father shared a headstone in one corner. Around the foot of Aunt Daisy's tall cross were all sorts of plants and mementos brought by reverential Girl Scout troops from all over the nation.

I remembered Mother once making it clear that she preferred Bonaventure, a more manicured cemetery on the other side of town. "This one seems a bit rundown," she murmured. "Never mind," Father reassured her. "By the time we need it, we'll be a bit rundown ourselves." It was Father, too, who advised me to regard Laurel Grove just as an anteroom to eternity, "a pleasant place to rest until you're told which way you're supposed to go."

Sitting there in the warm sunshine, it occurred to me that perhaps in the South death is woven more closely into the fabric of living than it is in other parts of the country. I have often seen cars stop on country roads and the occupants get out and stand respectfully, hats in hand, while the funeral cortege of some total stranger winds slowly by.

Funerals themselves seem to have more flavor, too. I remember the night in New York when a phone call came from Savannah to tell us Miss Sophie had died. Miss Sophie was a truly great lady, admired and loved by all for her wit and charm. The caller said he hoped that I could come back and be a pallbearer. Miss Sophie herself had wished it.

I had some meetings of great importance the following day, so I said that I was afraid it was not possible. Then I hung up the phone, and sat there feeling worse and worse. Finally I called back and said I would get on a plane that same night and come down.

And I was glad I did, because somehow it was a joyous occasion. As we came back down the aisle of the church with Miss Sophie's coffin, the organist threaded a few bars of "Dixie" into the recessional. At the cemetery, Miss Sophie had arranged for a bagpiper to be stationed in a nearby grove of trees, playing a wild Celtic lament. She also had the minister read a passage from "John Brown's Body" that seemed just right. Then we all went back to Miss Sophie's house where she had pre-planned a festive lunch, complete with champagne. We raised our glasses in the old toast, "To absent friends." But I did not feel that Miss Sophie was absent at all. She was right there enjoying everything with the rest of us.

The sun was getting hot, and it was time for my visit to Laurel Grove to end. I looked up, hoping to catch a glimpse of the old owl, but he was not there. I found myself listening too, and I did seem to hear, very faint and far away, one more verse of the old spiritual as Charlotte used to sing it:

If you get there before I do,
(Comin' for to carry me home)
Tell all my friends I'm a-comin' too.
(Comin' for to carry me home)
Swing low. . . .

Nothing gloomy or depressing about that, is there? Just some plans for a long-desired reunion and the arrival of a gleaming celestial conveyance that will take you, absolutely free, from where you are to where you want to be—home.

And One
for the Road

We Americans live in a youth-centered culture, not much doubt about that. People shy away from the thought of death, and even from the inevitability of growing older.

Here is the Irish poet William Butler Yeats speaking:

> *An aged man is but a paltry thing,*
> *A tattered coat upon a stick, unless*
> *Soul clap its hands and sing, and louder sing*
> *For every tatter in its mortal dress.*

Clap hands and sing? It is not easy for the soul to do this as the years go by and vitality begins to wane. In my own case, I have found a conflict raging inside my head between acceptance of the limitations that age brings and a determination not to let them interfere too much with the bright-colored patterns and habits of the past.

Of course, the birthdays keep coming. Here's what Yeats has to say about that:

> *The years like great black oxen tread the world,*
> *And God the herdsman goads them on behind. . . .*

In the end, the great black oxen will prevail. But before they do, I have found, there is a kind of twilight time when one can still follow many of the old paths if one is lucky and reasonably careful, and not put off by all the cautionary impulses that raise their frowning heads: "Better not try this any more." "Don't risk that." "You should know better at your age."

For example, I have always been a fisherman, and a surf fisherman at that. One can look for Reality in all sorts of ways (and never quite touch it), but for me a very close approach is to stand knee-deep or waist-deep in foaming saltwater, with sunrise ahead of me and a deserted beach behind me, and no sounds save the hum of the wind and the hiss of the foam and the plaintive cries of the gulls.

Of course, once you are past eighty, if you go by yourself to your sandbar in a small boat, there are some risks involved. Mishaps can occur. Prudence warns you to stay home or at least take a like-minded companion with you. But such companions are not always available. What then? To go or not to go? Does soul clap its hands or sit in a rocking chair?

The story that follows offers no final answer, but I can recognize myself in it. And yes, once upon a time, I did have a raggedy dog named Andy.

Not Far From Sundown

The old man came out of the Medical Arts building and walked down to his car where the small black dog waited, paws on window sill, ears up, brown eyes following every movement. A ragged tail thumped the upholstery.

"Move over, Andy," the old man said. He sat for a while gripping the wheel with hands that were thin but still strong. He looked up at the fierce sunlight gilding the weather vane on the courthouse down the street. "Ever had a cardiogram, Andy? Well, don't."

The old man had had others, of course, but this was the first since the blackouts had started, annoying little lapses, very quick, where darkness seemed to come at him from the outside corners of his eyes and everything faded but then gradually brightened again. He had said nothing to Martha—why alarm her?—but since she was away for a few days visiting the grandchildren, he had decided to let the doctor check it out.

Now he almost wished he hadn't, because the verdict and the sentence were discouraging. No undue stress or excitement. No sudden exertion. Specifically, no more solitary expeditions down the lonely windswept beaches. "I know it'll be tough," the doctor said, "for you to give up surf fishing and messing around with boats. But slow-down time comes to all of us. Besides, you've already caught most of the fish in the sea, haven't you?"

It was one of those questions designed to make you feel better that somehow managed to make you feel worse.

"I suppose the man is right, Andy," the old man said. "But it's pretty annoying when a bunch of electric wires can tell you what to do. Look at that weather vane. Southeast wind; high tide around noon. One more little excursion won't make much difference, probably; why don't we try it before Miss Martha gets back and tells us we can't?"

In the little tidal river, the skiff was riding thirty yards offshore. The old man flicked his surf rod so that the three-ounce sinker arched out and the leader wrapped itself around the anchor line close to the bow. He reeled in slowly until the keel of the skiff touched bottom, then looked at the dog sitting at the water's edge. "Come on, Andy," he said, "be brave. You may not be able to swim, but you can wade, can't you?"

Andy stood up, touched one paw to the water, then sat down again, looking dejected.

The old man sighed, picked Andy up, and deposited him in the boat. "Not only are you a coward," he said, "you're also the ugliest dog on the Eastern seaboard. Even your tail is hideous. How did I ever get stuck with a wretched beast like you?"

Andy looked up and wagged his hideous tail. He knew a compliment when he heard one.

The dog, just a stray which had been found half-starving beside a road some years ago, now went everywhere the old man went, even in the boat, although it was clear that some unknown early trauma had left him with a profound fear of water. Once the old man had tried to overcome that fear, placing the dog on a tiny sandbar with a rising tide and the boat not ten feet away. But the misery in Andy's eyes as the water rose was more than he could stand, and in the end he put the dog back in the skiff where he sat motionless, like a misplaced black fireplug, until they were home and the old man carried him safely to shore.

Now he sat in just such fashion as the skiff drove through the chop in the middle of the river, and then on through the network of creeks on the far side, where terrapin skittered down the muddy banks and mullet swirled in the green water and the great blue herons soared up and away. The old man watched these things with a certain intensity, as if trying to imprint them on his mind.

They came at last to a broad estuary flowing eastward through the barrier beaches with leaping tongues of surf on either side where it met the sea. A short distance upstream from this entrance was a little cove, and here the old man anchored the boat, placing Andy carefully ashore and watching him chase sandpipers, barking wildly. He never yet had caught one, and never would, but the old man understood how he felt. A dream is just a belief in possibilities, however remote, and this was Andy's dream.

He circled back at last to bark even more fiercely at a horseshoe crab, stranded on its back in a shallow pool, legs moving faintly. Seeing this, the old man paused. "Don't be rude to that crab, Andy," he said. "His ancestors were on this earth long before yours or mine. Besides, if we speak nicely to him and help him out, the sea gods may reward us." He picked up the grotesque creature by its armored tail, feeling life vibrating within it still, and carried it back toward the estuary with the dog pacing uneasily alongside. "Your mistake, Andy," he said, "is treating this crab as if it were an it, instead of thinking of it as a you. Try to get the notion through that head of yours that every living creature is a you, just as you are. Took me a long time to figure that out, but it sort of ties things together somehow. So let's just say, 'Good luck to you, old crab,' " and he tossed it out into deep water while Andy stared, bemused.

On then through some shallow dunes where the sea oats nodded to their own shadows and across the broad beach, blinding white in the sun, with scattered driftwood and bundles of marsh grass and bleached sanddollars. Two hundred yards offshore, gulls were mewing and diving where some ravenous mackerel were tearing up a school of baitfish. No other human being was in sight, no houses, no manmade thing, except far off against the dunes the rusted engine of a wrecked shrimp boat. The old man knew that very few beaches like this could be found anywhere, and that this one could not remain untouched for very long. But he tried not to think about it.

Near the water's edge, he put his gear on the sand and sat down beside it, waiting for his heart to cease its pounding. Ahead of him was a shallow lagoon or slough with the tide easing into it from one end, and beyond that a narrow sandbar where the big rollers broke with a sound like a muffled thunder.

Andy came up, panting, and the old man poured some water from a small thermos and gave him a drink. "Nice day, isn't it, Andy? Nice friendly day. Nobody's trying to run us off today. But that was a queer business last year, wasn't it? It scared you, I know, and spooked me too. Yessir, it did."

<hr />

They had been fishing in this place on a bright autumn afternoon, wind and tide favorable, water so clear you could see schools of mullet stacked up in each wave as it curled over to break. The old man had made a few casts, at peace with himself, at peace with everything, waiting to see what the sea had to offer. Andy was sitting, tired of chasing sandpipers, content to wait as long as necessary.

Then without warning the sun seemed to grow dim. The green water turned the color of lead. The wind died, but the air seemed colder. The birds vanished. A ringing silence settled over everything. Waist deep in the warm water, the old man felt the hair on the back of his neck tighten. He looked quickly, left and right, for a shark's fin, and then behind him. Nothing. But the feeling of isolation and dread grew stronger. On the beach Andy had crouched down suddenly like a dog expecting an undeserved blow. *This is nonsense,* the old man thought, but a deeper part of him knew that it was not nonsense. Something invisible was surrounding him, crowding in, something enormous, something very powerful, very threatening. That something was laying claim to the special solitude of this place, and it did not want to share it with any human being. Or any dog, either.

The old man had tried to close his mind against a rising tide of panic. He started backing up, reeling in, but suddenly the line was slack. He felt no strike, no tug, nothing, but he knew that hook and leader and sinker were gone. He turned then and splashed fast through the lagoon, back to the beach where Andy was still crouched beside the tackle box. He scooped up his gear and started back to the skiff, the dog close at his heels, angry with himself for fleeing but with a sense of near terror that was stronger than his anger. He put the dog in the boat, snatched up the anchor, cranked the engine, opened the throttle wide and roared westward up the estuary. And he did not look back.

◇———◇

His pulse seemed to be running steadily and easily now, so he reached for his tackle box and took out a pair of pliers. "If this is the last roundup, Andy, why don't we even the odds a bit?" Picking up the hook at the end of the long leader, he carefully mashed the barb flat. "May cost us a fish or two, but that's all right." He took a piece of cut mullet and inserted the now barbless hook so that the needle point went through the skin at one place and came out at another. He stood up a bit stiffly. "Now," he said to Andy, "if you had an ounce of loyalty, you'd swim this lagoon and join me on the bar. But I know you won't. Why couldn't I have a noble retriever named Rex or something instead of a misbegotten mutt like you?"

Andy lay down and put his nose on his forepaws. He judged words by tone, not content, and knew that all was well.

The old man waded across the lagoon, climbed the short steep bank on the far side, and moved into the surf until the breakers swirled about his knees. The silver scales of the mullet glittered as the line soared out into deeper water. In a short time the bar would be covered and the lagoon would be five feet deep. But the old man knew he had an hour of fishing before that, perhaps a bit more.

For ten minutes he waited, feet braced against the thrust of the waves, cap brim pulled down over his eyes to lessen the sun dazzle. A flight of pelicans came by, coasting downwind. Beyond the breakers, the gleaming black backs of two porpoises surfaced and disappeared. The wind blew and the foam seethed softly and the tide moved in.

Abruptly, with a tremendous shock, something seized the line. The rod bent almost double, then sprang erect again as a black-tipped shark, close to five feet, exploded into the air in a frenzy of spray, threw the hook, and was gone.

The old man felt his heart lurch with the sudden rush of adrenaline. He stood quite still until it seemed quiet, then reeled in slowly. As he rebaited the hook, he noticed that his hands were trembling, so he waited another half minute before making his second cast. Then he moved back six paces and waited again, because some instinct in him knew that the shark was only a prelude.

He knew this with certainty, and so he was not surprised when something picked up the bait gently and stealthily and started moving out to sea. He had disengaged the brake on the reel and was controlling the line only with his thumb, so he was able to apply pressure very gradually. But the pressure made no difference, the bait kept moving out until he knew he would have to begin to fight the fish before the line was all gone. So he flipped on the brake and struck hard.

It was like setting the hook into a runaway locomotive. The reel gave a metallic screech, the line was ripped off despite the drag. The old man felt the tremendous pressure on his arms and shoulders, and he knew that this pressure must be maintained or the barbless hook would slip out and the fish would be gone. By aiding the drag with his thumb—and getting it burned—he managed to slow the first tremendous straightaway rush of the fish, but he could not stop it. He knew that somehow he would have to turn it, eventually. If it began to swim laterally, he might be able to move with it and begin to recover some line. Already he could see the linen backing through the few turns of monofilament left on the reel, and so he began to walk forward, following the fish. The water rose to his shoulders. A wave lashed him across the face and knocked off his cap. He still held the rod high and the strain was becoming unbearable when, far out, he saw the long dark shadow of his adversary silhouetted inside a towering roller, saw too the angry flash of a great bronze tail that could belong only to an enormous channel bass—stag bass, redfish, a fighter by any name.

The old man decided that he would either turn the fish or break the line. He put most of his remaining strength into a desperate heave, and the head of the fish swung round, and it began to swim parallel to the beach, moving toward the point where the mouth of the lagoon met the incoming tide. The old man knew that he would never be able to land such a fish in the heavy surf; his only chance was to maneuver it into the lagoon itself. And after twenty minutes, that is what he did, backing up slowly, hearing his own breath come in gasps, gaining ten feet of line and losing twenty, always keeping the tension on the fish until finally he could see it in the calm waters of the lagoon, where it made two or three last convulsive runs and then rolled over on its side, fins and tail moving faintly.

The old man waded forward slowly, feeling his knees tremble, keeping the rod tip high and the line taut. He came to the great fish and knelt beside it, knowing the queer mixture of triumph and regret that comes at such a time. He saw that the hook was embedded in a corner of the wide mouth, not far down the throat as he had feared. He said in a murmur, "You're pretty tired, aren't you, old fish? Believe me, so am I." He reached forward and removed the hook, which slid out easily, but the exhausted bass made no lunge for freedom. It lay there, its yellow eye regarding its captor remotely.

"You'd like deeper water, wouldn't you?" the old man said finally. He put his rod down on the bottom of the lagoon—something he hated to do—and slid his arms under the passive fish. He eased its great weight gently out to a point where the water was four feet deep. He cradled it in his arms just under the surface, where the sunlight glinted on the gill-plates opening and closing and the mother-of-pearl flanks and the massive tail with its two black spots. He waited, and gradually the fish righted itself as its strength came back. At last it pulled away and began to swim, slowly at first, then faster and faster, toward the mouth of the lagoon and the open sea.

The old man stood up and watched it go. He turned, intending to look for the rod he had left under water, but suddenly he felt dizzy and knew he had better get back to the bar while he could. He was within three feet of it when the darkness swept over him, and he fell face down on the dry sand with his legs and feet still in the waters of the lagoon.

How long he lay there he did not know. Finally, a shallow

wave swirling across the bar slapped him in the face and he raised his head, choking and gasping. The darkness receded then and he came up on one elbow, glancing back toward the beach where his tackle box and spare rod rested tranquilly above the high-water mark. There was no sign of Andy, but when the old man sat up and scanned the now choppy waters of the lagoon, he saw a small black head moving toward him, ears flattened, eyes showing white with fright, submerged altogether now and then, but still coming, still swimming, closer and closer until the old man was able to reach forward and draw the shivering little animal into his lap. "Well done, Andy," he said. "I don't know how you thought you could help me, but I thank you for trying."

They sat there quietly for a little while. With his coat slicked back and his brown eyes, Andy looked almost like a baby seal. The old man could feel the dog's heart hammering furiously. "Well, come on now," he said. "Better go back before it gets any deeper. Don't be afraid. I've got you and you've got me. We'll make it all right."

And so they did, the old man moving slowly through the current with one arm around Andy, holding his head up until they came safely to the beach and made their way back to the skiff and home together. The old man wondered if from now on Andy might be a swimmer, but when they came to their final anchorage and he invited his companion to jump over and wade ashore, the invitation was declined. "Never mind, Andy," his master said, carrying him to shore. "We've had a good day. A very special day, don't you think?"

He tossed out the anchor and stood for a moment watching

the skiff swing wide. One of the things he liked about his boat when she rode at anchor was the calm unhurried way, no matter which way the current ran, she always faced the tide.

That evening when he called Martha, as he did every night when they were separated, the old man said nothing of what the day had held. It would keep until she got home. In fact, he thought, as he climbed wearily into bed and switched off the light, he might not tell anyone. Somehow it all might stay more intact if he didn't. He would know and Andy would know and that would be enough.

Andy was tired too. He went over to his scrap of carpet in the corner and lay down with a boneless thump. The old man smiled as he heard him sigh. He closed his eyes then, and at once, against the blackness inside his eyelids, the great bronze fish swam through green and gold depths, striped now by shadow, tail and fins moving silently, remote and untroubled in the element where it belonged. Farther and farther away it moved, growing smaller and smaller until, with a final mother-of-pearl flicker, it was gone, and sleep came down like a benediction, and the long day was over.

And so the story ends with the old man safe in his bed, although perhaps some readers thought he was not going to make it. Actually he's still alive, a little closer to sundown perhaps, but sitting right here at his old Corona manual typewriter wondering why it seems to take so much longer to put words on paper than it did sixty years ago. One reason may be that where words are concerned something inside him is harder to please, so that when he writes a paragraph nowadays he instantly thinks of a dozen ways to make it better. This may result in smoother prose, but it can also lead to increasingly diminished production if you don't watch out.

Well, never mind, it has been a wonder-filled journey ever since the far-off day when that small boy waited for the ice wagon to come over the dunes or rode spellbound in the cab of locomotive Number 1560. And now if the sun hangs low in the sky, that is nothing to fret about, is it? Sometimes a sunset can have a quiet splendor, a quiet wonder, of its own.

Return to Wonder was originally published by the book division of the company that publishes *Guideposts,* a monthly magazine filled with true stories of people's adventures in faith.

Guideposts is not sold on the newsstand. It's available by subscription only. And subscribing is easy. All you have to do is write to Guideposts, 39 Seminary Hill Road, Carmel, New York 10512. When you subscribe, each month you can count on receiving exciting new evidence of God's presence, His guidance and His limitless love for all of us.

Guideposts is also available on the Internet by accessing the homepage on the World Wide Web at http://www.guideposts.org. Send prayer requests to Monday morning Prayer Fellowship. Read stories from recent issues of their magazines, *Guideposts, Angels on Earth, Guideposts for Kids* and *Positive Learning,* and follow the popular book of daily devotionals, *Daily Guideposts.* Excerpts from some of their best-selling books are also available.